Bloom's
GUIDES

Carson McCullers'
The Member of the Wedding

1984
The Adventures of Huckleberry Finn
All the Pretty Horses
Beloved
Brave New World
The Chosen
The Crucible
Cry, the Beloved Country
Death of a Salesman
The Grapes of Wrath
Great Expectations
Hamlet
The Handmaid's Tale
The House on Mango Street
I Know Why the Caged Bird Sings
The Iliad
Lord of the Flies
Macbeth
Maggie: A Girl of the Streets
The Member of the Wedding
Pride and Prejudice
Ragtime
Romeo and Juliet
The Scarlet Letter
Snow Falling on Cedars
A Streetcar Named Desire
The Things They Carried
To Kill a Mockingbird

Bloom's
GUIDES

Carson McCullers'
The Member of the Wedding

Edited & with an Introduction
by Harold Bloom

CHELSEA HOUSE
PUBLISHERS
A Haights Cross Communications Company
Philadelphia

First Printing
1 3 5 7 9 8 6 4 2

Library of Congress Cataloging-in-Publication Data

Carson McCullers' The member of the wedding / edited and with an introduction by Harold Bloom.
    p. cm. — (Bloom's guides)
 ISBN 0-7910-8172-9 (alk. paper)
 1. McCullers, Carson, 1917-1967. Member of the wedding. I. Bloom, Harold. II. Series.
 PS3525.A1772M53 2004
 813'.52—dc22

                                                    2004014458

Chelsea House Publishers
1974 Sproul Road, Suite 400
Broomall, PA 19008-0914

www.chelseahouse.com

Contributing editor: Cathy Schlund-Vials
Cover design by Takeshi Takahashi
Layout by EJB Publishing Services

Every effort has been made to trace the owners of copyrighted material and secure copyright permission. Articles appearing in this volume generally appear much as they did in their original publication with little to no editorial changes. Those interested in locating the original source will find bibliographic information in the bibliography and acknowledgments sections of this volume.

Contents

Introduction

HAROLD BLOOM

I met Carson McCullers two or three times during the late Fifties and early Sixties. More than forty years later, I still retain a visual memory of her eyes, which seemed almost too vivid, large, and young in a countenance that reflected many psychic and physical sufferings.

I have just finished a rereading of her four major fictive works: *The Heart Is a Lonely Hunter*, *Reflections in a Golden Eye*, *The Ballad of the Sad Café*, and *The Member of the Wedding*, which I had experienced for the first time when it was published in 1946. I was sixteen, and shy enough to empathize deeply with the twelve year old Frankie. After almost sixty years, I hardly can recall my other early impressions of the book. Rather unfairly, it had to compete with Thomas Hardy's *The Woodlanders*, which I read almost simultaneously. Hardy had little in common with McCullers, though his disciple, D.H. Lawrence did. One could nominate Lawrence's *The Rainbow* rather than Faulkner's *The Sound and the Fury* as the masterpiece of her mode, though Faulkner was an overt influence, and the vitalistic Lawrence was not.

The Member of the Wedding is the most carefully composed of McCullers' narratives, and like *The Heart Is a Lonely Hunter* and *The Ballad of the Sad Café* probably is a permanent book. McCullers is not the peer of Flannery O'Connor or even of Eudora Welty: she cannot break free of her autobiographical context in her best work, and the failure of *Reflections in a Golden Eye* indicates that she had to stay within herself to write effectively. Yet *Clock Without Hands* seems too auto-biographically obsessed to work, and shows that McCullers had reached an impasse. Whether she could have attained a new phase, had she not died at fifty, is difficult to judge.

The Member of the Wedding deserves its popularity, and is much more than a period piece. Like *The Heart Is a Lonely Hunter*, it reaches out to what is most yearning in the common reader. The gatherings of Frankie , Berenice, and John Henry, as they eat and play cards together, are memorable in many ways, and their conversations are poignantly humorous. All three are rendered as persuasive and endearing personalities, and Frankie is a more complex and evocative version of Mick Kelly, perhaps because the style of Carson McCullers is more nuanced in the later book. There is no splendor of longing in Mick or in Frankie, but both of them possess an authentic aesthetic dignity. Through them, McCullers added an individual accent to the immemorial human need to risk false connections in the quest to overcome loneliness.

Biographical Sketch

For Southern writer Carson McCullers, the segregated neighborhoods, textile mills, and busy main streets of her childhood home of Columbus, Georgia would provide the inspiration, setting, and foundation for her later literary works. Lula Carson Smith (Carson McCullers) was born on February 19, 1917, the oldest child of Marguerite Waters Smith and Lamar Smith. McCullers was a precocious child who spent the long, hot Georgia summers exploring and playing in Columbus's backyards and shaded avenues. McCullers had two younger siblings—her brother Lamar, Jr. and her sister Margarita—and together they enjoyed a comfortable middle class existence in the thriving industrial center of Columbus, which was located at the falls of the Chattahoochee River near the Alabama state line.

McCullers' father Lamar, who would serve as the inspiration for John Singer in *The Heart is a Lonely Hunter* and Frankie Addams's father Royal in *The Member of the Wedding*, was a successful jeweler of French Huguenot ancestry. The youngest of ten children in an Alabama farming family, Lamar had come to Columbus as a young man to work as a watchmaker in a jewelry store, which he later owned. Her mother, a housewife, was a longtime resident of Columbus. Marguerite was convinced that her eldest daughter was a childhood genius and focused her attentions on fostering McCullers' artistic development. These efforts were initially focused in the area of music, and McCullers began studying the piano at the age of five, practicing between five to six hours a day. By McCullers' twelfth birthday in 1930, she had learned everything her instructor in Columbus could teach her, and she began taking lessons from Mary Tucker, a gifted pianist and wife of an army colonel at nearby Fort Benning. It was also at this time that McCullers changed her name from "Lula" to "Carson." Two years later, when McCullers was fourteen, she suffered from pneumonia and undiagnosed rheumatic fever, and these serious illnesses, in hindsight, would serve as a harbinger of the health problems that would plague McCullers in her adult life.

When McCullers was fifteen, her father had given her her first typewriter, and later McCullers maintained that, by that age, she had written three plays. In later interviews, McCullers proclaimed that she had composed her "first short story" at the age of seventeen. The title of this piece, "Sucker," was written from the point of view of a sixteen-year-old named Pete. The work focused its narratival attention on Pete's affair with a girl by the name of Maybelle and the impact of this affair on his relationship to his younger brother, who he calls "Sucker." Pete has, in pursuing Maybelle, abandoned the affections of his younger brother. At the conclusion of the story, Pete has lost both Maybelle and the love of his brother, and it is this issue of loss—along with the guilt and frustration associated with it— would later be echoed in McCullers' major literary works.

In addition to her literary pursuits, McCullers was a dedicated musical practitioner who, when she graduated from high school at the age of seventeen, decided that she would further her study in New York City at the prestigious Julliard School of Music. McCullers had, like her protagonists Mick Kelley in *The Heart is a Lonely Hunter* and Frankie Addams in *The Member of the Wedding*, always wanted to go North, and Julliard provided both escape and a fulfillment of that desire. In order to afford Julliard's tuition, the family sold her grandmother's diamond and emerald ring, and McCullers moved to New York City in 1934. However, McCullers' time at Julliard was short-lived—her roommate had lost her tuition money, and McCullers was forced to take odd jobs in the city to support herself. It was at this point that McCullers decided to pursue writing on a more serious level, and she enrolled in night classes at Columbia and New York University where she studied with Helen Rose Hull, Sylvia Chatfield Bates, and Whit Burnett. Hull, Bates, and Burnett were important mentors to the young McCullers—Burnett and Bates in particular would prove instrumental in fostering her career as a published writer.

McCullers, over the course of 1934–1936, divided her time between New York City and Columbus, Georgia because of poor health. It was during this period that two significant events took place—one professional in scope, the other personal. While taking writing classes in New York City, McCullers wrote an autobiographical short story about a fifteen-year-old girl's discovery during a music lesson that she is not the prodigy she had thought herself to be. This story, entitled, "Wunderkind," impressed Whit Burnett, who in 1936 published it in the notable literary magazine *Story*. That same year, during a return visit to Columbus, McCullers met James Reeves McCullers, a corporal in the army who also had literary aspirations. The following year, in September 1937, the two married and moved to Charlotte, North Carolina, where Reeves, who had left the army, took a temporary job as a credit manager.

While in North Carolina, McCullers found that she had few distractions, and, for the first time in her life she was able to devote all of her energy to writing a novel that she had been planning for months. Originally entitled *The Mute*, this work would later be named *The Heart Is a Lonely Hunter* at the suggestion of her publisher. As the novel neared completion, McCullers sought the advice of Sylvia Chatfield Bates, who told her to send the completed part of her manuscript and an outline to Houghton Mifflin. The publishing company awarded McCullers a fellowship of $1,500 to complete the manuscript, and *The Heart is a Lonely Hunter* was accepted for publication in 1939, appearing in print the following year. The novel's setting, which takes place in a small Georgia mill town during the 1930s, was largely based on McCullers' childhood observations and experiences in Columbus, Georgia. *The Heart is a Lonely Hunter* describes the efforts of five lonely people to break out of their respective isolated states and make contact with the larger, apathetic outside world. Thus, at the young age of twenty-three, McCullers had successfully entered the realm of the published writer, and the novel enjoyed wide critical acclaim. She was compared to Ernest Hemingway, John Steinbeck, Thomas Wolfe, and William Faulkner; in the *New York Times Book Review*, influential critic Rose Feld asserted that McCullers "writes with a sweep and certainty that are overwhelming"[1].

The success of *The Heart Is a Lonely Hunter* allowed Reeves and McCullers to relocate to New York City. However, the professional success McCullers enjoyed was not mirrored in her personal life, for soon after the couple moved McCullers decided to file for divorce, following a series of complicated extramarital relationships undertaken by both Reeves and McCullers. In the summer of 1940, McCullers and the editor of *Harper's Bazaar*, George Davis, rented an old brownstone house in Brooklyn Heights. This brownstone, which would later be known as February House, served as an important site for authors and artists, and became a twentieth-century version of the 1840s literary and social commune Brook Farm. Literary luminaries such as W.H. Auden, Truman Capote, and Tennessee Williams frequented February House, as did Gypsy Rose Lee. McCullers made February House her home for the next five years, though she did make frequent outings to Yaddo, the writer's colony in Saratoga Springs, and back to Georgia.

The year 1940 also saw the completion of McCullers' second novel *Reflections in a Golden Eye*, a text that explored the tribulations of a latently homosexual army captain. *Reflections in a Golden Eye* was published the following year in February of 1941, but did not enjoy the same critical acclaim as McCullers' previous work. In the winter of 1940, while in Columbus, McCullers suffered the first in a series of strokes that would haunt her for the remainder of her life. This first stroke temporarily impaired her vision, and it took McCullers two months to recover. McCullers, in the early stages of recovery, wrote the short story, "A Tree, A Rock, A Cloud" that was published in *Harper's Bazaar* in November 1942, and selected soon after by Herschel Brickell for inclusion in the anthology *O. Henry Memorial Prize Stories of 1942*. McCullers' divorce from Reeves was finalized earlier that year, and Reeves re-enlisted in the army to fight in World War II. That same year, McCullers was awarded a Guggenheim Grant and a $1,000 award from the American Academy of Arts and Letters, which gave her the opportunity to work on a novel that would eventually become *The Member of the Wedding*.

McCullers had resumed her relationship to her ex-husband Reeves, who was at this time stationed overseas. The two shared a steady correspondence over the next two years, and they would, in 1945, remarry after Reeves was discharged from the army for an injured wrist. Reeves and McCullers would periodically live in Nyack, New York with McCullers' mother. McCullers suffered two more strokes in Paris in 1947 that destroyed the lateral vision in her right eye and left her left side paralyzed. McCullers, in poor health, returned to New York at the end of the year. She would, for the next few years, travel back and forth between Nyack, New York, New York City, and Paris. However, as McCullers was experiencing success from the publication of *The Member of the Wedding*, her personal life was growing more problematic. After the war, Reeves had given up his aspirations to become a writer and soon began to drink. His alcoholism made married life increasingly difficult, and he was often subject to abusive episodes and suicidal thoughts, and had, at one point, tried to convince McCullers to participate in a double suicide attempt. In 1953, while McCullers was away from Paris, Reeves ended his life with an overdose of sleeping pills.

McCullers had, soon after the start of the Broadway production of *The Member of the Wedding*, begun work on a new novel, *Clock without Hands*. Reeves' suicide in 1953 and her mother's death in 1955 interrupted McCullers' writing of the new novel. In an attempt to contextualize the traumatic events of the past few years, McCullers wrote a play, *The Square Root of Wonderful*, which opened on Broadway October 30, 1957. Unlike *The Member of the Wedding*, this second dramatic work did not enjoy the same stage success, and it closed five weeks later. McCullers then returned to writing *Clock without Hands*. Because of physical illness and depression, the work took another three years to complete, and it was finally published in the spring of 1961, almost ten years after it was begun. *Clock without Hands*, McCullers' last novel, was not a critical success. McCullers spent the year following the publication of *Clock without Hands* in a wheelchair, and her next work—a collection of children's poems entitled *Sweet as a Pickle and Clean as a Pig* was published in 1964. McCullers' health continued to fail—she was diagnosed with breast cancer in 1962, and she had series of strokes. In the midst of illness, McCullers' *Reflections in a Golden Eye* was optioned for cinematic adaptation. Directed by John Huston and starring Marlon Brando and Elizabeth Taylor, the film version began production in 1966, and was scheduled for release the following year.

McCullers would not live to see the release of this latest cinematic adaptation of her work. Bedridden since 1964, on August 15th, 1967 Carson McCullers suffered a major cerebral hemorrhage, which affected the right side of her body. A little over a month later, on September 29th, McCullers died as a result of complications associated with the stroke. She was fifty years old.

The Story Behind the Story

McCullers had begun writing *The Member of the Wedding* shortly after the publication of *Reflections in a Golden Eye* in 1941, and the novel would take her five years to complete. She interrupted her writing of *The Member of the Wedding* in 1943, when she spent six months writing *The Ballad of the Sad Café*, a novella focused on the love affair between a hunchbacked dwarf and a giantess. *The Ballad of the Sad Café*, like *The Heart is a Lonely Hunter*, received critical acclaim, and further solidified her status as a significant American writer of the 1940s.

Originally entitled "The Bride" and then "The Bride and Her Brother," McCullers agonized over the various stages in writing of the work. For example, according to biographer Virginia Spencer Carr, the scope of the novel's plot and nature of the protagonist's struggle were particular points of consternation for McCullers. After months of conceptualizing the novel's structure, McCullers came to a decision after an outing with Gypsy Rose Lee. While drinking coffee and brandy with Lee, McCullers heard the sirens of a fire engine in her neighborhood and the two chased the engine for several blocks. Suddenly, McCullers stopped Lee and shouted, "Stop! I have it! Frankie is in love with her brother and the bride and wants to become a member of the wedding!" (*Understanding Carson McCullers* 73). The process of writing, however, was still slow-going for McCullers; she spent her time constantly revising the work because, as she revealed in a letter to Reeves, she felt that "It's one of those works that the least slip can ruin.... It must be beautifully done. For like a poem there is not much excuse for it otherwise."[2]

The Member of the Wedding was eventually completed and published in 1946, close to a year after McCullers and Reeves had remarried. The work enjoyed both critical and commercial success, and McCullers, soon after its publication, received another Guggenheim fellowship. Tennessee Williams, upon reading the novel, asked to meet McCullers, where he urged her to consider adapting the novel into a play. Williams later

15

invited McCullers to spend a few weeks with him at his summer cottage in Nantucket and, as Williams wrote *Summer and Smoke*, McCullers worked on rewriting *The Member of the Wedding* for the stage. The first version of the play adaptation was completed at the end of the summer, and McCullers and Reeves sailed to Europe in the fall of 1946

Though New York directors and producers were wary of the work's viability on the stage, the play version of *The Member of the Wedding* opened on Broadway on June 5, 1950 and enjoyed a successful run. The following year, in 1951, an edition of collected works, published under the title *The Ballad of the Sad Café*, was positively and enthusiastically reviewed by critics, further solidifying her status as an American writer. In 1952, the film version of *The Member of the Wedding* was released (an adaptation from the successful Broadway play).

List of Characters

Frankie Addams is the protagonist of the novel, and as the narrative opens, she is an inquisitive, precocious, and naïve twelve-year-old girl. In the beginning of *The Member of the Wedding*, Frankie is isolated from both her family and her friends, and she searches for connectedness. This journey to find a place of belonging centers on her brother Jarvis's upcoming wedding, which will, according to Frankie, give her the opportunity to simultaneously start a new life and escape her present-day small town Southern existence. Situated between childhood and adolescence, Frankie negotiates her feelings of loneliness and dislocation over the course of the novel, and this process is manifest in the various identities she assumes in the three parts of *The Member of the Wedding*. For example, she initially calls herself "Frankie," then, in the second section, she uses the name "F. Jasmine." In the concluding part of the novel, she takes on the name "Frances." Each name signals a shift in Frankie's self-conceptualization of herself as a young adult, and her story represents a coming-of-age narrative.

Berenice Sadie Brown is the Addams' African American housekeeper who, since her first marriage to Ludie Freeman ended when he passed away, has been married to three other men. She is quite open about her various relationships, discussing them with both Frankie and John Henry. Berenice also reveals, in her discussions with Frankie, the inequalities between African American residents and their white counterparts. She provides a voice of reason to Frankie's fantastical imagination and naivete. Berenice points out the ways in which Frankie's projections and ideas often contradict the reality of her and her brother's respective situations.

John Henry West is Frankie's six-year-old first cousin who spends much of the novel at the Addams' house. Though only a child, John Henry has a maturity that goes beyond his years, and he often counters Frankie's irrational behavior with a calm disposition and an insightful perspective. His sudden death from meningitis is quickly mentioned and briefly discussed at the conclusion of *The Member of the Wedding*.

The Soldier remains unnamed in *The Member of the Wedding*. On leave for three days, the soldier is in town and is staying at the Blue Moon, the local hotel and saloon. A sullen figure, the soldier is often drunk and uncommunicative. His interest in Frankie is sexual in scope, though Frankie is not immediately aware of his intentions.

Royal Quincy Addams is Frankie's father whose wife, Frankie's mother, died when Frankie was born. He owns a jewelry shop in town, where he spends the majority of the novel. His presence in the narrative is minimal yet undeniable. Frankie's sense of dislocation is in part due to her father's insistence that, because she is older, she must sleep by herself.

Jarvis Addams is Frankie's older brother. At the beginning of *The Member of the Wedding*, Jarvis is about to marry Janice Evans in the nearby town of Winter Hill. Absent from the real time action of the novel, Jarvis is represented in flashback moments. Jarvis, who is in the military, was at one point stationed in Alaska, and Frankie spent that time fantasizing about her brother's life far from the town in which she lives. Frankie imagines that Jarvis and his soon-to-be wife will provide an escape from her home. Jarvis, for the most part, is revealed in the text vis-à-vis flashback moments.

Janice Evans is Jarvis's fiancee from Winter Hill, and, like Jarvis, she is mostly revealed in flashbacks.

Barney Mackean was a friend of Frankie's with whom she shared an intimate moment. According to Frankie, the two of them had "committed a queer sin" in the Mackean's garage, and it is the memory of this moment that haunts Frankie and causes her to feel shame. Frankie's reaction to both Barney and this particular memory further reinforces the sense that she is unable and unwilling to recognize her own sexuality and impending adulthood.

Uncle Charles is John Henry's great uncle who, after a long illness, dies on the Saturday before Jarvis and Janice's wedding. Frankie initially reacts adversely to the news of his death, fearing that it will overshadow the wedding and, by connection, her plans to leave.

Evelyn Owen was Frankie's best friend who has moved away to Florida. Her absence in Frankie's life is one of the factors behind Frankie's assertion at the beginning of the novel that she was "a member of nothing in the world."

Honey Brown is Berenice's foster brother who lives with Big Mama. Described by Big Mama as "unfinished," Honey is an unstable figure in the novel, and he, like Frankie, seems to be searching for both meaning and a place. At the conclusion of *The Member of the Wedding*, it is revealed that he has been sent to jail as a consequence of a failed store robbery, which was committed when Honey was under the influence of marijuana.

T.T. Williams is Berenice's current love interest who works in a restaurant in town. Financially secure and stable, Berenice is initially reluctant to marry him. However, at the conclusion of the novel, Berenice does agree to marry T.T.

Ludie Freeman was Berenice's first husband, who died the same year Frankie was born in 1931. Berenice tells Frankie that Ludie was the love of her life, and that she has spent the years after his death trying to recapture his presence and that feeling.

Big Mama is Berenice's mother. Big Mama is the local fortuneteller, and Frankie visits her prior to the wedding. Frankie asks Big Mama to read her fortune, and Big Mama tells her that she will go on a trip and return. Frankie is unhappy with the reading, for it undermines her fantasy of leaving home. As the conclusion of the novel reveals, Big Mama's prediction comes true—Frankie does remain in the town.

Mr. and Mrs. Marlow were boarders in the Addams household. They were evicted after Frankie witnesses the two of them sharing an intimate moment, though Frankie is unaware of the actuality of what has happened. According to Frankie, Mrs. Marlowe was "having a fit," and though it is not explicitly mentioned, it can be assumed that the couple was engaged in sexual intercourse. Frankie's inability to determine the exact nature of their actions further emphasizes her sexual naïveté.

Aunt Pet and Uncle Ustace are Frankie's relatives who are mentioned but do not make an appearance in the novel. At the conclusion of *The Member of the Wedding*, Frankie and her father are preparing to move into a suburban house with Aunt Pet and Uncle Ustace.

Mary Littlejohn is introduced in the final section of *The Member of the Wedding*. She is two years older than Frankie. By the end of the novel, Mary Littlejohn is Frankie's closest friend. Her appearance at the conclusion of *The Member of the Wedding* signals to the reader that Frankie now belongs to a particular group and that she has become a "member" of the community in which she lives.

Summary and Analysis

The Member of the Wedding takes place in a small Southern town in Georgia. The novel begins on the last Friday in August 1944. The central plot line focuses its narratival attention on Frankie Addams (the protagonist) and traces her complicated journey from childhood into young adulthood. From a structural standpoint, the novel is divided into three parts, and the story is primarily told from a third person point of view, through the voice of an unidentified narrator. Though a third person point of view, the narrator is not entirely objective; the perspective provided by the narrator is mediated through the protagonist's thoughts, desires, and past experiences. And, it should also be noted that the narration is not consistent in terms of diction and tone. The protagonist changes names and identities in each of the three sections of the novel and the third person narration style in each of these sections follows these changes accordingly. There are also moments of dialogue interwoven within the work, and this gives the reader a more objective perspective on the events that take place through the course of the novel.

Part One opens with the following description by the unidentified narrator:

> It happened that green and crazy summer when Frankie was twelve years old. This was the summer when for a long time she had not been a member. She belonged to no club and was a member of nothing in the world. Frankie had become an unjoined person who hung around in doorways, and she was afraid.
> (*The Member of the Wedding* 3)

The use of the pronoun "it" initially dislocates the reader, for it is unclear as to the subject of the narrator's revelations. However, as the narrative continues, this pronoun becomes much more defined and expanded, and is repeated throughout the first section of *The Member of the Wedding*. As is quickly revealed in the next few paragraphs and dialogue excerpts, "it" refers to Frankie's brother's upcoming wedding, which serves as a focal point for the narrative. The wedding serves as a catalyst for action in the novel, prompting the protagonist to explore her own desires for connectedness and inclusion, along with her fears about adulthood and her voyage into adolescence. On another level, "it" can also be read as a reference to the coming-of-age moments that characterize Frankie's experiences throughout the novel, and can thus be seen as a pronoun that encapsulates the narrative in its entirety.

Moreover, as the paragraph continues, the unidentified narrator establishes, from the outset, Frankie's lack of connectedness. Prior to the start of the novel, Frankie has been isolated, "a member of nothing in the world ... an unjoined person." As Part One progresses, the reasons for Frankie's feelings of disconnectedness become apparent—her mother died while in childbirth, leaving her father a widow. Earlier that summer, Frankie's father has told her that she is too old to sleep next to her father and is forced to sleep alone. Moreover, her best friend, Evelyn Owen, has moved away to Florida, and the older teenage girls in her neighborhood refuse to play with her. And, the news of the wedding—the pairing of her brother with another person—provides another possible instance of exclusion. This lack of membership to any group or any person further establishes the significance of the title of the novel, which can be read as a direct reference to the protagonist, whose story dominates the narrative.

Moreover, as the narrator reveals, Frankie is, at least at the outset, unable to fully comprehend the news of her brother's wedding, which is scheduled to take place the last Sunday in August. The narrator, at the end of the first paragraph of Part One, asserts that the news of the wedding seemed "so sudden that Frankie puzzled the whole blank afternoon, and still she did not understand" (*The Member of the Wedding* 3). It is this inability to comprehend the meaning of the wedding that becomes apparent in the beginning moments of the conversation between Frankie, Berenice Sadie Brown, and John Henry West—the three primary characters in *The Member of the Wedding*. The scene that follows the narrator's initial observation takes place around the table in the Addams's kitchen, a setting that will be revisited and re-staged multiple times throughout the novel with the same gathering of characters.

The action of the novel begins with a conversation about the upcoming wedding, and this discussion takes place at four o'clock in the afternoon over a game of three-hand bridge. Frankie comments on the "queerness" of her brother and his fiancé, who have visited prior to the start of this scene. Berenice confronts Frankie, asking if she is "jealous." Given that Frankie is, in the initial moments of *The Member of the Wedding*, disconnected and isolated and a member of nothing, such an observation is insightful, for it alludes to Frankie's envy of her brother and his bride, who are connected and about to be joined in matrimony. This joining is juxtaposed with the earlier mention by the narrator of Frankie as an "unjoined person." The narrator provides a physical description of Frankie within this scene, and this description re-enforces Frankie's "outsider" status. According to the narrator,

> This summer she was grown so tall that she was almost a big freak, and her shoulders were narrow, her legs too long. She wore a pair of blue track shorts, a B.V.D. undervest, and she was barefooted. Her hair had been cut like a boy's, but it had not been cut for a long time and was now not even parted ... (*The Member of the Wedding* 4)

The notion that Frankie was "almost a big freak" alludes to the fact that Frankie is entering pubescence and is in the midst of a growth spurt. The detail of her hair, which "had been cut like a boy's" refers to the sense that Frankie is both a tomboy and is still stuck in childhood. Thus, Frankie, at the beginning of *The Member of the Wedding*, is located mentally and physically on the brink of childhood and adolescence, and her inability to understand the implications of her brother's impending nuptials is a manifestation of her location between these two points.

Moreover, Frankie confirms Berenice's observation that she is "jealous" with her assumption that her brother and his bride-to-be "have a good time every minute of the day," revealing that, unlike her, they are experiencing excitement and activity. As the conversation continues, Frankie, Berenice, and John Henry play cards, and the narrator provides a physical description of each character, yet it is important to note that these descriptions, like the one of Frankie that has preceded them, is rendered from Frankie's perspective and privileges her relationship to both Berenice and John Henry. For example, the narrator asserts that "Berenice had been the cook since Frankie could remember," which contextualizes her vis-à-vis Frankie. The narrator continues to describe Berenice as "very black and broad-shouldered and short" and that "there was only one thing wrong with Berenice—her left eye was bright blue glass" (*The Member of the Wedding* 5). The image of this eye, along with the motif of seeing, is revisited multiple times in the novel, and Berenice's insights—which often counter Frankie's lack of comprehension—are linked metaphorically to this notion that Berenice can see beyond superficial realities. John Henry, the last character to be described by the narrator, was "blood kin to Frankie, first cousin," a child who wore "tiny gold-rimmed glasses" (*The Member of the Wedding* 5) and, though half Frankie's age, (he is six-years-old) he can like Berenice, see through Frankie's motives and through the course of the novel, counters Frankie's reactions with a calm and keen perspective.

As the three characters play cards, Frankie reiterates the "suddenness" of the news, and it is revealed, by the narrator, that Frankie has in the recent past fantasized about her brother's life. Her brother, a corporal in the army, had been stationed in Alaska, a place so fantastical to Frankie that she "had dreamed of it constantly" (*The Member of the Wedding* 6). The narrative then jumps to a moment prior to the start of the novel, when Frankie, the day before her brother and his fiance's visit, tells Berenice that she wishes she didn't have to return to her home town after the wedding; instead, Frankie wishes that she "was going somewhere for good" (*The Member of the*

Wedding 7). Berenice counters Frankie's announcement with an observation that Frankie seems to wish for a lot of things. Frankie then responds with a more telling statement, asserting to Berenice that she wishes that she "was somebody else except me," which signals, to the reader, Frankie's discomfort with both her life and her self.

The narrative returns to the present, and chronologically follows the conversation in the kitchen. It is the early part of the evening. Frankie invites John Henry to stay for dinner and spend the night, and this invitation comes from Frankie's fear, which the narrator asserts she is unaware of causes. Berenice asks Frankie why she extended the invitation, stating that she had, in the past, expressed her boredom with him as a playmate. Frankie claims that she asked John Henry to stay because he seemed "scared," and when pushed further by Berenice to clarify the source of his fear, Frankie replies, "Maybe I mean lonesome" (*The Member of the Wedding* 8). This exchange is significant in that Frankie is the one who is "lonesome," and the invitation is made to assuage her fear of loneliness. John Henry, later that evening, comes over to stay over, and he and Frankie commence to making men out of the biscuit dough set aside for dinner.

Frankie, John Henry, and Berenice eat supper at the kitchen table. It is important to note the absence of Frankie's father, Royal Addams, from this dinner dynamic. Royal had called earlier to inform Berenice that he would be working late in his jeweler's shop and would not join them for dinner. This detail is significant for it illustrates the extent to which Frankie is isolated from her family—her mother, who died in childbirth, is a figure she has never known.[3] Her brother Jarvis has been, as previously mentioned, been stationed in Alaska and has, for the past two years, been absent from Frankie's life. And, her father, her closest immediate family member, spends most of his time away from Frankie at work. This disconnectedness from her father is further re-enforced by the fact that, as previously mentioned, Royal has told his daughter that she must sleep alone because she is too old to sleep in his room. Royal's literary absence from the novel (he is briefly mentioned and inconsistently appears) mirrors his absence in Frankie's life, providing yet another reason for Frankie's intense sense of loneliness.

In the background, a radio is on, and the narrator reveals that it is "playing a mixture of many stations: a war voice crossed with the gabble of an advertiser, and underneath there was the sleazy music of a sweet band" (*The Member of the Wedding* 9). Though briefly mentioned by the narrator in this instance, World War II is an undeniable presence in the novel. The setting of the novel temporally occurs toward the end of World War II, and, alongside Frankie's burgeoning awareness of herself as a young adult is her sense of a larger world outside of her immediate community. Moreover, other characters in the novel, namely the figure of the soldier (who appears in the second part of *The Member of the Wedding*) and Frankie's brother Jarvis are integrally linked to the war effort as members of the military. Frankie's self-located sense of uncertainty is echoed on the national stage—the American war effort abroad was, in 1944, in the midst of stasis, with no clear path to victory.

After Frankie, Berenice, and John Henry finish dinner, Frankie asks John Henry what he would like to do, and he tells Frankie that "There's a big crowd going to play out tonight" and suggests that they join this crowd. Frankie tells John Henry that she doesn't want to follow this suggestion, and then, after John Henry pushes her to go out, gets angry and tells him that this group is "just a lot of ugly silly children" (*The Member of the Wedding* 9). This furthers the sense that Frankie is conflicted and alienated. On the one hand, Frankie has invited John Henry, a six-year-old boy, to stay with her overnight; on the other hand, Frankie doesn't want to interact with a group of "silly children," and, given her isolation from other groups (the details of which are given later in the section), she is also fearful of not belonging. After this exchange, Frankie and John Henry go to her room to unpack John Henry's weekend bag, and he asks Frankie if she would prefer he go home. Frankie tells him to stay, and the narrative then shifts from a two-character dialogue to an interior monologue rendered by the narrator.

In this moment of the narrative, Frankie imagines two objects—a lavender seashell and a glass snow globe, and thinks about venturing to the Gulf of Mexico and Alaska respectively. Frankie, unlike John Henry (who has been to Birmingham) has not yet traveled and has never seen snow. This imagining, coupled with Frankie's desire to leave and join a larger world sphere, foreshadows Frankie's later declaration, at the end of the Part One, to join her brother and his new bride after the wedding. On another level, John Henry's experience—with both snow and with Birmingham—serve as reminders to Frankie that she has yet to experience life in the world, and this experience is, at least for most of the novel, connected to Frankie's simultaneous fascination and fear with the unknown.

In continuing with this particular scene, Frankie remembers, as the result of John Henry's assertion that the "big girls are having a party in their clubhouse," that she is no longer a member of this club and has been relegated to a bystander status. According to the narrator, the girls, who were thirteen, fourteen, and fifteen years of age, had told Frankie that she was "too young and mean." Frankie, after this rejection, "sometimes ... went around the alley behind the clubhouse and stood near a honeysuckle fence." Frankie, upon hearing the news about the party, reacts negatively and suddenly, screaming to John Henry that he not "mention those crooks to me" (*The Member of the Wedding* 10). Interestingly, the choice of "crooks" corresponds to Frankie's sense of loss, which is embedded in the multiple renunciations and denials of inclusion she has witnessed from her father and her peers. John Henry insightfully states that they may "change their mind and invite you," further illuminating that the source of her dislike for the group is rooted in the denial of an invitation. Frankie attempts to buttress her claim that the girls were dishonest by telling John Henry that they had spread untrue rumors about her around town and "were talking nasty lies about married people" (*The Member of the Wedding* 11). This last statement about "married people" is never fully contextualized; however, given Frankie's fears about sex and sexuality, which are revealed in the later portions of Part One, these "nasty lies" may be linked to discussions of sex.

John Henry and Frankie prepare for bed, undressing with their backs to one another. According to the narrator, "with somebody sleeping in the dark with her, she was not so much afraid" (*The Member of the Wedding* 13). Thus, the loneliness that has both characterized this particular summer and haunted Frankie is, because of John Henry's presence, temporarily assuaged. The novel then takes the reader into the next morning, on Saturday, the day before the wedding, and Frankie, John Henry, and Frankie's father Royal sit in the kitchen as Berenice cooks breakfast. The narrative then subtly shifts from the present to the past, to the day that Frankie's brother Jarvis and his fiancé Janice visit and Frankie finds out that the two are planning to marry. The flashback is prompted by the similarity of setting; in other words, it was a morning like this one that Frankie finds out about her brother's impending nuptials, yet the news of this has had a great transformative impact. The impact of this news is fully realized in the latter portion of Part One, when Frankie reveals her desire to join the couple after the wedding.

Prior to this revelation, the narrative moves from this flashback to a later moment on Saturday. Frankie, Berenice, and John Henry are playing a game of cards, and it is 5:45 p.m. Thus, the narrative has skipped over an entire day. John Henry, through the course of the game, does not play by the rules—he refuses to place a jack of spades next to the queen of spades. He tells Berenice that he doesn't "want to play my jack under Frankie's queen" and asserts that he will not do it. Frankie dismisses John Henry as a "child" (*The Member of the Wedding* 14) and tells Berenice that she is sick. According to the narrator, the sight of the cards made Frankie sick; more specifically, the narrator maintains that the three of them (Berenice, Frankie, and John Henry) "had played cards after every dinner every single afternoon.... if you would eat those old cards, they would taste like the combination of all the dinners of that August ..." (*The Member of the Wedding* 14). It is significant that Frankie has such a reaction to the cards. The playing of cards has become a routine, and it is this routine, and the monotony it embodies, that causes Frankie's reaction. Frankie's boredom and irritation with the cards is juxtaposed with her enthusiasm and anticipation of the wedding, which, according to the narrator, "was bright and beautiful as snow" (*The Member of the Wedding* 14). This image hearkens back to a previous moment in Part One, when Frankie imagines how exciting a life in Alaska would be and wishes that she would be able to see snow and experience the larger world.

The narrative shifts from the narrator's ruminations to a dialogue between Frankie, Berenice, and John Henry. Frankie tells Berenice and John Henry that both her brother's and his bride's first names begin with "J A" and wishes that her name could also being with those letters, and puts forth "Jane" and "Jasmine" as possibilities. Berenice interrupts and tells Frankie that she heard on the radio that the French are chasing the Germans out of Paris, and Frankie asks if it is against the law to change one's name. Berenice responds that it is, and Frankie asserts that she doesn't care and renames herself "F. Jasmine Addams." Incidentally, it is this name that Frankie uses in Part Two of *The Member of the Wedding*, and it symbolically marks a shift from Frankie's identity in the first section to the more adult, yet still naïve, persona in the second part of the novel. In following this identity shift, Frankie gives John Henry one of her dolls to keep, and this act can be read as emblematic of Frankie's desire to shed her childhood.

Frankie then looks into the kitchen mirror and states that she wishes she had not gotten a crew cut and that she should have "long bright yellow hair" for the wedding. While looking in the mirror, the narrator reveals to the reader that Frankie was afraid, and the narrative shifts its focus to Frankie's height. More specifically, Frankie had grown four inches in the past year, and the children in her neighborhood have been teasing her about her height. Frankie attempts to mathematically predict her height at the age of eighteen, and she thinks she may grow over nine feet and would be "a Freak" (*The Member of the Wedding* 16). This thought prompts Frankie to reflect back to a time she was at the local fair and visited the House of the Freaks. Frankie was afraid of the "freaks" and was worried that, because of her growth, she will soon be "one of them." According to the narrator:

> She was afraid of all the Freaks, for it seemed to her that they had looked at her in a secret way and tried to connect their eyes with hers, as though to say: we know you. She was afraid of their long Freak eyes. And all the year she had remembered them, until this day.
>
> (*The Member of the Wedding* 17)

Interestingly, the above passage represents a mode of membership for Frankie, yet this membership is not desired and in fact precipitates anxiety and fear. After this flashback moment, the narrative returns to the present, and Frankie, Berenice, and John Henry continue their discussion in the kitchen. Frankie whispers to Berenice, asking her if she thinks she will grow into a "Freak"; Berenice tells her "certainy not, I trust Jesus", which makes Frankie feel better.

The discussion then returns to the wedding, and Frankie expresses a desire to "improve herself" before the wedding. Berenice tells her wash up, and Frankie "looked for a last time at herself in the mirror, and then she turned away." According to the omniscient narrator, Frankie "thought about her brother and the bride, and there was a tightness in her that would not break" (*The Member of the Wedding* 18). This moment of introspection represents Frankie's inability to understand the gravity of her brother's wedding. And, on another level, this reaction, along with the thoughts and remembrances that precede it, illustrates Frankie's insecurities about her physical appearance and her frustration with her current life. This sense is re-enforced by the narrator's assertion that

> This was the summer when Frankie was sick and tired of being Frankie. She hated herself, and had become a loafer and a big no-good who hung around the summer kitchen: dirty and greedy and mean and sad.
>
> (*The Member of the Wedding* 18).

The narrator further contextualizes Frankie's feelings of alienation, and, in the process, reveals that the year has been marked by a sense of transition and change for the protagonist. For example, the narrator maintains that

> It was the year when Frankie thought about the world.... She thought of the world as huge and cracked and loose and turning a thousand miles an hour.... Frankie read the war news in the paper, but there were so many foreign places, and the war was happening so fast, that sometimes she did not understand....
>
> (*The Member of the Wedding* 419)

Frankie's re-conceptualization of the outside world anticipates her shift from childhood into young adulthood, and she begins to see the complexities and issues that accompany a life in the adult world. It is also revealed in this section of the novel that Frankie, in an attempt to link up to the war effort, tries to donate blood to the Red Cross, only to be denied because of her age. It should be noted that Frankie initially wished she was a boy so that she could go to war as a Marine, but realized that this was not a possibility and elects instead to go to the Red Cross. Frankie interprets this denial from the Red Cross as yet another club from which she has been excluded, and she is afraid of the war not because of "Germans or bombs or Japanese. She was afraid because in the war they would not include her and because the world seemed somehow separate from herself" (*The Member of the Wedding* 20). It is this fear of exclusion that dominates Frankie's sense of self in Part One of the novel.

And, it is because of exclusion that Frankie has sought, according to the narrator, a life outside of the town, and it is her sense of loneliness that causes the "tightness in her chest." In an effort to break out of this loneliness, Frankie "did things and she got herself in trouble." It is revealed that she repeatedly "broke the law"—one time she took her father's pistol and shot it in a vacant lot; another time, she stole a "three-way knife" from the local Sears and Roebuck Store. Yet, it is the final "crime" enumerated that is perhaps the most significant. The narrator mentions the incident with Barney MacKean, when Frankie committed "a secret and unknown sin," one that "made a shriveling sickness in [Frankie's] stomach" and caused her to "drea[d] the eyes of everyone" (*The Member of the Wedding* 21). Though not explicitly mentioned, the incident with Barney may have been sexual in scope, and Frankie's discomfort with its occurrence coincides with her reluctance to speak about sex and sexuality (as in the previous case with the "big girls" and the "nasty lies about married people"). Frankie eventually distances herself from this moment, but it will be revisited later in the novel, when Frankie meets the soldier.

The narrator continues to mention the elements of Frankie's life prior to the scenes at the kitchen table on the last weekend in August. It is revealed that Evelyn Owens, Frankie's best friend, moved away to Florida that year, and Frankie "did not play with anybody any more" (*The Member of the Wedding* 21). The narrative then shifts to the Sunday "when it happened, when her brother and the bride came to the house" and it is this moment that "Frankie knew that everything was changed; but why this was so, and what would happen to her next, she did not know" (*The Member of the Wedding* 22). Frankie is initially unable to name the reason why the thought of the wedding gives her a "kind of pain"; however, given that Frankie has spent most of the summer in isolation and "unjoined," the news of the wedding, as mentioned previously, carries with it the possibility of further exclusion.

The narrative then shifts to a conversation between Frankie and Berenice. Frankie asks Berenice how old she was when she married her first husband; Berenice tells Frankie that she was thirteen years old. The narrative moves again to a third person narration, and it is revealed that Berenice had been married four different times. According to the narrator, who is rendering the story from Frankie's perspective, Berenice's husband, Ludie Freeman, was the best of the four. The narrator mentions that Berenice and Ludie had "gone to Cinicinnati and seen snow ..." and the snow image, as in other instances, symbolizes to Frankie a level of freedom she currently does not enjoy. After nine years of marriage, Ludie had passed away, and Berenice's other three husbands were abusive. The narrative returns to the conversation about Berenice's past relationships, and Frankie, feeling restless, grabs a butcher knife. Frankie then asks Berenice to tell her what happened when Jarvis and Janice came to visit, and Berenice tells Frankie that

> Your brother and the bride come late this morning and you and John Henry hurried in from the back yard to see them. The next thing I realize you busted back through the kitchen and run up to your room. You came down with your organdie dress on and lipstick a inch thick from one ear to the next. Then you all just sat around up in the living room. It was hot. Jarvis had brought Mr. Addams a bottle of whisky and they had liquor drinks and you and John Henry had lemonade. Then after dinner your brother and the bride took the three o'clock train back to Winter Hill. The wedding will be this coming Sunday. And that is all. Now, is you satisfied?
>
> *(The Member of the Wedding* 24)

Berenice, in the above passage, provides a summary for both Frankie and the reader about the details surrounding the revelation of Jarvis and Janice's upcoming wedding. Interestingly, Berenice is the one who provides the most coherent and direct account of the news; unlike the narrator, who refers to the wedding with the pronoun "it," and Frankie, who has, up to this point, mentioned only the fact that it will happen, Berenice provides a complete listing of the day the wedding news was announced. Additionally, Berenice, in mentioning that Frankie had her "organdie dress on" and lipstick, points out that Frankie attempted to look older than she was and "pass" as an adult. Berenice, in making this observation, reveals that Frankie is, though almost the same age as she was when she married Ludie, still very much a child. And, as Berenice's account reveals, the adults had "liquor drinks" while Frankie and John Henry had lemonade, further emphasizing that Frankie is more closely connected to John Henry.

Frankie and Berenice continue to discuss the upcoming wedding, and Frankie asks Berenice to provide more details about both the day of her brother's visit and what will happen after the wedding. The narrative shifts to the beginning days of August, and more facts emerge about Frankie's life prior to the opening of the novel. More specifically, Frankie's cat Charles had disappeared, and this occurrence has prompted Frankie to tell Berenice on a daily basis that "It looks to me like everything has just walked off and left me" (*The Member of the Wedding* 26). However, this routine is broken the day before the wedding, when Frankie calls the police and reports his disappearance to the police. It is significant that Frankie uses the name "F. Jasmine Addams" in her report for it signals a shift in the way Frankie conceptualizes herself. Moreover, the use of this name, which will become more frequent in Part Two of *The Member of the Wedding*, represents a new identity for Frankie, one that attempts to encapsulate her newfound association as a particular member of the wedding. This association is revealed in the final pages of Part One.

Prior to this revelation, however, the narrative continues with Frankie and Berenice's conversation about the upcoming wedding. Berenice teases Frankie, telling her that she has a crush on the wedding; this taunting angers Frankie, who raises the knife and, after Berenice demands that she put it down, throws the knife at the kitchen door. Frankie then tells Berenice that she will be leaving town after the wedding. Berenice does not believe her, and questions her further about her plans, pointing out that she does not know where she will be going. The scene ends with the arrival of T.T. Williams, Berenice's current beau, and her foster brother Honey, who take Berenice home.

The narrative then shifts to the empty house, and Frankie's remembrances of Mr. and Mrs. Marlowe, who were, at one time, boarders in the Addams house. Frankie had caught Mrs. Marlowe "having a fit," and the two boarders were told to leave soon after. Frankie does not understand what exactly was happening between Mr. and Mrs. Marlowe, though it can be assumed, given the reactions of both Berenice and her father, that the two were engaged in sexual intercourse. Frankie's inability to contextualize what happened furthers the sense that she is both sexually naïve and unaware in Part One. The memory ends, and the narrative returns to the present, with Frankie unable to stay in the lonely house. She walks to John Henry's place and tells him that she doesn't want to return home alone. In the midst of their conversation, the narrative shifts from a dialogue to an interior monologue, and Frankie's thoughts are the focal points of this section. Frankie thinks about her brother and his fiancé, and then comes to the conclusion that *"they are the we of me"* (*The Member of the Wedding* 35).

It is this conclusion that both ends Part One and promulgates the action in Part Two of *The Member of the Wedding*. In stating that "they are the we of me," Frankie connects herself physically and emotionally to her brother and his fiancé; in the process, Frankie conceptualizes herself as part of a unit, and thus breaks, at least at this moment in the novel, the routine of exclusion that has characterized her recent life. This statement also provides an answer to the question of "who she was and what she would be in the world" (*The Member of the Wedding* 38), and it can be argued that it is the answer to this question that Frankie has been seeking in Part One of the novel. This association with her brother and his bride locates Frankie within a particular framework in which Frankie is recast as an integral and not peripheral figure in the wedding. And, this new role gives Frankie, least in her own mind, a substantive connection to the larger world and assuages the fear of isolation and loneliness that has previously circumscribed her twelve-year-old existence.

Structurally speaking, and unlike Part One, **Part Two** is divided into three chapters. **Chapter One, Part Two** begins with the statement, "The day before the wedding was not like any day that F. Jasmine had ever known" (*The Member of the Wedding* 41). It is important note that this section of the novel begins with Frankie's new identity—"F. Jasmine"—and that it is, from the outset, a day "not like any day," which counters the descriptions of routine that characterize Part One. Interestingly, though this was "not like any day," the narrative takes the reader to a time that was, in Part One, skipped over— the period of Saturday that spans from early morning until 5:45 in the evening. Thus, the reader is brought back to a moment that actually precedes the ending of Part One; on another level, the reader is given a further context for the protagonist's realization that her brother and his fiancé are "the we of me." It is important to remember, however, that the identity of "F. Jasmine" does temporally precede Frankie's conclusion about her connection to her brother and his fiancé, yet structurally and thematically this section seems to closely follow Part One.

F. Jasmine represents a markedly different manifestation of the protagonist than "Frankie"—more specifically, F. Jasmine is much more confident and certain of herself than "Frankie." For example, according to the narrator, "It was the old Frankie of yesterday who had been puzzled, but F. Jasmine did not wonder any more; already she felt familiar with the wedding for a long, long time" (*The Member of the Wedding* 42). Thus, unlike Frankie, F. Jasmine is not afraid but confident, nor is she filled with questions. Instead, F. Jasmine has a high degree of agency, and is a character of action. Part Two is written from this viewpoint.

In this particular section, the reader is also given a more detailed description of Royal Addams, and it is revealed that "he was a widowman, for her mother had died the very day that she was born ..." (*The Member of the Wedding* 43). Before Royal leaves for work, F. Jasmine tells her father that she will not be coming back after the wedding, receiving no response from her father. F. Jasmine then tells her father that she will have to buy a "wedding dress and some wedding shoes and a pair of pink, sheer stockings" (*The Member of the Wedding* 43). This statement, which is intended to evoke a further response from Royal, has more weight given F. Jasmine's decision to join her brother and his bride after the wedding. Though it is understood by her father that she needs to purchase these items as a peripheral part of the ceremony (e.g. as an audience member), the statement could also be read as F. Jasmine's desire to dress herself like the bride and take a more central role in the wedding ceremony. Royal doesn't vocally respond; instead, he gives signals his permission by nodding affirmatively.

F. Jasmine returns to the topic of her leaving after the wedding ceremony, and she tells her father that she will write him letters. Her father, however, does not acknowledge F. Jasmine's plans, or her transformation, and instead focuses his attention on his tool set—he lectures her about using his tools. F. Jasmine then leaves the house and ventures into town. The narrative moves from the house to the town, as F. Jasmine walks through the surrounding neighborhoods to the main street. The narrator focuses on F. Jasmine's newfound confidence and perspective, and the ways in which this newer identity causes the protagonist to see the world around her nostalgically, almost as if she has already left and has only recently returned. For example, when F. Jasmine sees main street, the narrator notes that it seemed "like a street returned to after many years, although she had walked up and down it only Wednesday" (*The Member of the Wedding* 45). And, it should be noted that the narrative is rendered through this new perspective; as is the case in Part One, the narration in Part Two is written according to the protagonist's thoughts and feelings. Put another way, whereas Part One is written to reveal Frankie's fears and the sources of these fears, Part Two is written from a more confident perspective that is much more assured and is more focused on the present and not the past.

When F. Jasmine reaches the town center, she searches for people to tell about her plans to leave town with her brother Jarvis and his bride. Interestingly, F. Jasmine feels connected with those around her, which counters the dominance of a disconnected sense in Part One. For instance, F. Jasmine sees "an old colored man, stiff and proud on his rattling wagon seat" and the two share a glance; according to the narrator, F. Jasmine "felt between his eyes and her own eyes a new unnamable connection, as though they were known to each other" (*The Member of the Wedding* 45). This narrative of connectedness is briefly interrupted with a moment from later that evening, when Berenice questions F. Jasmine about her connections to others, but quickly returns to the scenes in town. Though eager to tell those she sees about the wedding, it is not until she reaches the Blue Moon, a local bar, that F. Jasmine is able to share her news. According to the narrator,

> The Blue Moon was a place at the end of Front Avenue, and often the old Frankie had stood on the sidewalk with her palms and nose pressed flat against the screen door, watching all that went on there. Customers, most of them soldiers, sat at the boothed tables, or stood at the counter having drinks, or crowded around the juke-box.... There was no written law to keep her out, no lock and chain on the screen door. But she had known in an unworded way that it was a forbidden place to children. The Blue Moon was a place for holiday soldiers and the grown and the free. (*The Member of the Wedding* 47)

The Blue Moon as a site represents an adult world, one that "the old Frankie" could not enter because it was a forbidden place to children"; most significant, the Blue Moon is a place for soldiers, the grown, and the free, and F. Jasmine considers herself "grown and free" at this moment in the narrative. By entering the Blue Moon, F. Jasmine symbolically and confidently enters an adult realm.

As F. Jasmine enters the Blue Moon, the narrator notes that there was "the red-headed soldier who was to weave in such an unexpected way through all that day before the wedding" (*The Member of the Wedding* 48). This observation foreshadows a future meeting between the two characters, though at this moment the significance of this meeting is implied but not explained. F. Jasmine proceeds to the bar and orders a coffee from the owner behind the counter, who is referred to by the narrator as "The Portuguese." F. Jasmine tells the Portuguese bartender about her brother's upcoming wedding and her plans to leave the town following the ceremony. After telling the bartender her intentions, she "noticed ... for the first time ...

the soldier who at the very end would twist so strangely that last, long day." This second mention of the soldier is more detailed but the meaning of this observation is still not overtly apparent. After this revelation, the narrator further comments on the transformation that has taken place in the protagonist from Part One to Part Two; more specifically, the narrator (referring to the nonverbal interaction between F. Jasmine and the soldier) asserts:

> That morning, for the first time, F. Jasmine was not jealous. He [the soldier] might have come from New York or California—but she did not envy him. He might be on his way to England or India—she was not jealous. In the restless spring and crazy summer, she had watched soldiers with a sickened heart, for they were the ones who came and went, while she was stuck there in town forever. But now, on this day before the wedding, all this was changed; her eyes as she looked into the soldier's eyes were clear of jealousy and want.
>
> (*The Member of the Wedding* 49–50)

Thus, F. Jasmine, unlike Frankie, is characterized not by jealousy or envy but by a calm and self-assured demeanor. However, it is important to remember that Part Two actually chronologically precedes the last section of Part One, and that this persona is not permanent. In other words, F. Jasmine represents a particular state of mind that is not static but rather embedded in the process of becoming, which echoes adolescence, a time when one is in the process of becoming an adult. This motif of "becoming" is apparent in the transformation of "Frankie" to "F. Jasmine"; and, this transformation continues in Part Three with the protagonist's name change to "Frances," though it should be noted that this final re-naming is one enacted by the unidentified narrator and not by the protagonist.

Frankie leaves the bar and walks through various nearby neighborhoods and streets, looking other individuals to tell her story about the wedding. This episode is briefly interrupted with a parenthetical aside, which pushes the narrative to a later moment chronologically. This "future moment" takes place later that evening, when F. Jasmine/Frankie is telling Berenice about her day. Berenice incredulously responds to F. Jasmine/Frankie, and questions her on why she would think it was appropriate to tell such a story to strangers. The narrative then shifts back to F. Jasmine's trek through town. The protagonist walks to her father's store, and Royal tells her that Uncle Charles, the great-uncle of John Henry, has passed away. F. Jasmine attempts to answer in an adult manner, telling her father, "At one time Uncle Charles was one of the leading citizens. It will be a loss to the whole county" (*The Member of the Wedding* 54). However, Royal is unimpressed, and tells her to go back home. F. Jasmine reminds her father that she needs to get a wedding dress, and her father tells her go to a local store, MacDougal's. The protagonist leaves her father's jewelry store, and on the way to purchase a dress she spots "the monkey and the monkey-man" (an organ grinder and his pet monkey).

The man is engaged in an argument with the red-haired soldier, the one F. Jasmine had recently observed in the Blue Moon. The soldier has tried to purchase the monkey, despite the fact that the monkey is not for sale by the owner. The organ grinder and the monkey eventually escape from the soldier, who is angered by the exchange. F. Jasmine watches the scene and makes a comment about how she too had wanted to own a monkey. The soldier, who is drunk, asks F. Jasmine, "Which way are we going? Are you going my way or am I going yours?" and the two head back to the Blue Moon.

While at the Blue Moon the soldier buys F. Jasmine a beer, and she tells him about the wedding and her plans to leave. The soldier, for the most part, is unresponsive. He interrupts his silence with the question, "Who is a cute dish?" and F. Jasmine does not understand his meaning. The narrator observes, "There were no dishes on the table and she had the uneasy feeling he had begun to talk a kind of double-talk" (*The Member of the Wedding* 59–60). Though F. Jasmine does not understand the literal meaning of his question, she does sense its euphemistic nature. Thus, though the protagonist attempts to "pass" as an adult, she is still naïve about romantic relationships and romantic language. F. Jasmine does not comprehend both the soldier's meaning and his intention, which are both sexual in scope.

F. Jasmine attempts to redirect the conversation to a more comfortable point, and she continues to make small talk with the soldier. The soldier does not seem interested in this new direction, and F. Jasmine becomes increasingly uneasy. F. Jasmine decides to leave and she thanks the soldier for the beer. The soldier asks her to meet him for a date at nine o' clock that evening. F. Jasmine is conflicted—on the one hand, the date represents an entrée into adulthood; on the other hand, she understands that the soldier has mistaken her for an older woman. Though she initially says she does not know whether she can meet him, F. Jasmine eventually concedes.

As F. Jasmine walks home, the narrator reveals the shift in her attitude from earlier that day; more specifically, the narrator observes that the "passing walkers looked dark and shrunken in their angry glare." The narrator adds that "it took her a little while to come back to the wedding feeling of that morning, for the half-hour in the hotel had slightly distracted her frame of mind" (*The Member of the Wedding* 61). Interestingly, the confidence that characterized the first section of the chapter has now given way to shame, and it is important to note that this shame—which echoes the protagonist's memory of Barney Mackean in Part One—is embedded in a particular fear about sex.

According to the narrator, F. Jasmine does eventually "come back to the wedding feeling." While on her way to pick out a dress for the wedding, the protagonist runs into a younger classmate. She tells her classmate about her upcoming date, which signals a rethinking and recasting about the nature of her previous interaction with the soldier. However, according to the narrator, "the main thing that brought back the wedding frame of mind was an accident that occurred on the way home" (*The Member of the Wedding* 61). On her way home Frankie saw something sideways and behind her that had flashed across the very corner edge of her left eye; she had half-seen something, a dark double shape, in the alley she had just that moment passed. And because of this half-seen object, the quick flash in the corner of her eye, there had sprung up in her the sudden picture of her brother and the bride. Ragged and bright as lightning she saw the two of them as they had been when, for a moment, they had stood together before the living-room mantelpiece.... So strong was this picture that F. Jasmine felt suddenly that Jarvis and Janice were there behind her in the alley, and she had caught a glimpse of them—although she knew, and well enough, that they were in Winter Hill, almost a hundred miles away. (*The Member of the Wedding* 61–62)

This moment is significant in F. Jasmine/Frankie's later formulation that her brother and his fiancé are the "we of me." In the above passage, the narrator, rendering the scene from F. Jasmine's perspective, focuses on the relationship between the protagonist and the "dark double shape" in the alley, which reminds her of Jarvis and Janice. Although she knew they were in Winter Hill, F. Jasmine, in this moment, is convinced that they are with her in the alley, and that the three are connected spatially. Moreover, in this particular scene, the only three figures represented are F. Jasmine and the two shapes she initially thinks are Janice and Jarvis, and this configuration foreshadows F. Jasmine/Frankie's later revelation that the three are connected and will continue to function as a three-member unit after the wedding. In this moment, the divisions that exist between her brother and his bride as a matter of distance and age are briefly collapse. This vision is disrupted by F. Jasmine's realization that the two figures are not Janice and Jarvis and are instead two African American boys, "one taller than the other and with his arm resting on the shorter boy's shoulder" (*The Member of the Wedding* 62). The first chapter of Part Two concludes soon after the narrator's explanation.

Chapter Two, Part Two chronologically follows the previous chapter, and the narrative returns to the Addams's kitchen. F.

Jasmine returns home at two o' clock in the afternoon, and Berenice asks the protagonist where she has been for most of the day. John Henry is also in the kitchen, and he tells F. Jasmine about Uncle Charles's death. The three briefly discuss Uncle Charles's passing. F. Jasmine then asks why John Henry and Berenice "have to go tagging to the wedding" (*The Member of the Wedding* 63). Berenice responds, addressing F. Jasmine as "Frankie Addams," which prompts F. Jasmine to yell, "Don't call me Frankie!" This exchange further emphasizes the shift in the protagonist's self-conceptualization and re-enforces the sense that the F. Jasmine persona is distinct from "Frankie." It is important to note that other characters in the novel— Berenice, Royal Addams—do not acknowledge the more adult F. Jasmine. Furthermore, Berenice and Royal do not formally recognize the changes the protagonist attempts to reveal, which are embodied in the name change.

The fissures that erupt in the F. Jasmine persona are further revealed when Frankie tries to tell Berenice about the soldier. Berenice asks F. Jasmine if the soldier was drunk, and though this is apparent to the reader from the narrator's description of the soldier, it is not immediately apparent to the protagonist. F. Jasmine does not know how to respond to Berenice's question, for she finds it difficult to believe that someone would be drunk so early in the day. Berenice's question causes F. Jasmine to not reveal the full story of the soldier, and the protagonists redirects the discussion to the wedding. Berenice's question and F. Jasmine's response illustrate the extent to which F. Jasmine is still a child, one who cannot comprehend the realities of an adult world. F. Jasmine repeats that she will not come back after the wedding, and Berenice responds, asking the protagonist, "What makes you think they want to take you along with them? Two is company and three is a crowd. And that is the main thing about a wedding" (*The Member of the Wedding* 64). This question undermines F. Jasmine/Frankie's previous enunciation that Jarvis and his fiancé are "the we" of her. Berenice uses, as further proof of the assertion that "two is company and three is a crowd" with the parable of Noah and the Ark, in which animals were boarded in pairs. According to the narrator, "the argument that afternoon was, from the beginning to the end, about the wedding" and that Berenice "refused to follow F. Jasmine's frame of mind" (*The Member of the Wedding* 65). The protagonist, however, does maintain her position, in spite of Berenice's protestations to the contrary.

This moment in the narrative—the argument between Berenice and F. Jasmine—is reminiscent of a previous instance in the first chapter of Part Two. More specifically, when F. Jasmine first left the Blue Moon, after telling the Portuguese bartender her plans to leave after the wedding, there is a disruption in the narrative in which Berenice's disbelief is rendered, parenthetically, by the narrator. This section of *The Member of the Wedding* thus hearkens back to that moment and simultaneously brings the reader more fully into it. Berenice asks F. Jasmine what she will do if her plans to join her brother and his bride fail, and the protagonist answers dramatically, telling Berenice that she will shoot herself with her father's pistol. Berenice admonishes F. Jasmine for talking in such a manner. She then instructs the protagonist to go upstairs, and informs her that dinner will be ready shortly.

The narrative shifts to a familiar scene—F. Jasmine, Berenice, and John Henry are at the kitchen table, having dinner. According to the narrator, "It was a late dinner, this last meal that the three of them would ever eat together at the kitchen table" (*The Member of the Wedding* 66). From the outset, it seems as if the narrator is echoing the desires of the protagonist. This dinner takes place on Saturday, the night before the wedding. F. Jasmine has repeatedly asserted that she will leave after the wedding, and thus the narrator's statement seems to refer to this imagined "inevitability." Thematically speaking, the narrator's statement can be read through the transformation of the protagonist. Put another way, this dinner represents the last meal that F. Jasmine/Frankie will have at the table, for in the next section of the novel (Part Three), the protagonist, as briefly mentioned previously, will have a new name and a new identity as "Frances." There is yet another meaning to this statement, which becomes apparent at the conclusion of the novel. It is revealed in the final pages of the novel that John Henry, a couple of months after the wedding, dies from meningitis, and Berenice decides to marry T.T. Williams. These two events further make this gathering of the characters something of the past.

As F. Jasmine, Berenice, and John Henry continue to eat dinner, the conversation turns to the subject of love, and Berenice tells a story about a woman who fell in love with a man who later became a woman as the result of a sex change. F. Jasmine refuses to believe the story, in spite of Berenice's insistence of its validity. Berenice then tells F. Jasmine that "never before in all my days [have I] heard of somebody falling in love with a wedding" (*The Member of the Wedding* 68), and she comes to the conclusion that F. Jasmine needs a beau. F. Jasmine mentions the soldier and their date, though she does not specify that this is based in reality, and Berenice dismisses her talk of "soldiers and dancing" and instead suggests that F. Jasmine date someone like Barney Mackean. F. Jasmine answers in the negative, referring to him as "that mean nasty Barney," and the narration shifts from dialogue to a third person account of the protagonist's experience in the Mackean's garage. This moment, which was briefly mentioned in Part One, is revisited in more depth in the second chapter of Part Two. According to the narrator:

> The garage had been dark, with thin needling sunlight coming through the cracks of the closed door, and with the smell of dust. But she did not let her-self remember the unknown sin that he had showed her, that later made her want to throw a knife between his eyes. Instead, she shook herself hard and began mashing peas and rice together on her plate. (*The Member of the Wedding* 69)

Though not named, it can be inferred from the above passage that Barney and F. Jasmine shared an intimate moment that was sexual in scope. The protagonist's aversion to this memory mirrors her initial aversion and her reaction to the soldier's advances in the previous section. Though F. Jasmine attempts to pass as an "adult," a person of the world, her reaction to sex and sexuality are emblematic of her naiveté about matters of love and the actualities of adult relationships. Thus, her transformation from child to adult is still incomplete.

The narrative returns to the conversation, and John Henry asks Berenice about her beaus. Berenice tells F. Jasmine and John Henry about her past relationships. F. Jasmine disrupts the conversation and advises Berenice to "quit worrying about beaus and be content with T.T." and that "it is time for [her] to settle down" (*The Member of the Wedding* 69). Berenice immediately challenges her advice, and questions her authority on the subject. John Henry breaks the tension between Berenice and F. Jasmine by asking Berenice if all her beaus treated her to picture shows. The conversation about Berenice's past relationships continues and eventually segues into a discussion about foods.

F. Jasmine attempts to raise the subject of the soldier a second time; however, she is interrupted by the sound of a piano that is being tuned in the neighborhood. The narrator observes that

> In the silence of the kitchen they heard the tone shaft quietly across the room, then again the same note was repeated. A piano scale slanted across the August afternoon. A chord was struck. Then in a dreaming way a chain of chords climbed slowly upward like a flight of castle stairs: but, just at the end, when the eighth chord should have sounded and the scale made complete, there was a stop. The next to the last chord was repeated. The seventh chord, which seemed to echo all of the unfinished scale, struck and insisted again and again. And finally there was a silence. (*The Member of the Wedding* 71)

The tuning of the piano, and the incompleteness of the scale, mirrors F. Jasmine's attempt to tell the story about the soldier. After all, she has attempted to tell John Henry and Berenice the story and has twice been interrupted, and in the retelling of the story, she repeats the notes and has not had a chance to finish. On another level, this image of the incomplete piano scale takes on additional significance in relationship to the protagonist's development. F. Jasmine is still incomplete—though she attempts to pass as an adult, she is still a child, especially when it comes to the issue of relationships. Finally, the incompleteness of the scale also echoes the protagonist's incompleteness, which is linked to an initial disconnectedness. Though the protagonist asserts that she has, at least up to this point in the novel, reconnected herself and has found the "we" of her, this connection will only be complete *after* the wedding, which has not taken place.

F. Jasmine, after a short pause, asks Berenice whether or not she would go out with someone who struck her as "peculiar," and though the protagonist is framing the question around the soldier, she cannot provide Berenice more detail because, according to the narrator, "she could not further explain" (*The Member of the Wedding* 72). Berenice does not give her a definitive answer, telling F. Jasmine instead that it would depend on how she felt. The phone rings and John Henry picks it up, but when F. Jasmine takes the phone and speaks into the receiver, there is no response. Berenice then asks F. Jasmine to show her the dress and shoes she bought, and the protagonist puts on her wedding clothes and models them for Berenice and John Henry. Berenice disapproves of F. Jasmine's audacious outfit, which consists of an orange satin evening dress, silver shoes, and a silver bow, stating that "it don't do." When asked by F. Jasmine to specify the problems with outfit, Berenice points out the protagonist's crew cut and dirty elbows, which are incongruous with the adult evening dress.

John Henry interrupts the discussion about F. Jasmine's clothes, stating, "Uncle Charles is dead.... And we are going to the wedding" (*The Member of the Wedding* 75). This observation causes F. Jasmine to shiver and think

> back to the other seven people she knew. Her mother had died the very day that she was born, so she could not count her.... Then there was her grandmother who had died when Frankie was nine years old, and F. Jasmine remembered her very well—but with crooked little

pictures that were sunken far back in her mind. A soldier from that town called William Boyd had been killed that year in Italy.... Mrs. Selway, two blocks away, had died.... She knew Lon Baker, and he was dead also. Lon Baker was a colored boy and he was murdered in the alley behind her father's store.... She knew, but only in a chancing kind of way, Mr. Pitkin at Brawer's Shoe Shop, Miss Birdie Grimes, and a man who climbed poles for the telephone company: all dead. (*The Member of the Wedding* 75–76)

The above passage is significant in that it makes explicit mention of F. Jasmine's mother, who died "the very day that she was born" and is a figure the protagonist has never known. Thus, the protagonist's naiveté about adolescence and sex is partially attributable to the absence of a mother figure, though it can be argued that Berenice fulfills this role in the narrative. In addition, this passage further emphasizes the shift between the child-like personage of Part One to the more adult persona the protagonist embodies in Part Two. There is an intentional slippage of names—when the protagonist remembers the death of her grandmother, the narrator uses the name "Frankie" to refer to her nine-year-old self. The more adult "F. Jasmine" is also used in the same sentence, for it is this second manifestation of the protagonist who is reflecting and remembering those who have died. Interestingly, though this has yet to happen at this point in the novel, the protagonist will know, at the conclusion, another person who has died—John Henry.

This focus on death serves as a transition into another discussion between F. Jasmine, Berenice, and John Henry. F. Jasmine asks Berenice about her first husband, Ludie Freeman. Berenice maintains that her life with Ludie represented the best time of her life, and that all the bad husbands who have followed further re-enforce this notion. According to the narrator, "Of all the dead people out of the world, Ludie Freeman was the one F. Jasmine knew best, although she had never laid eyes on him, and was not even born when he had died" (*The Member of the Wedding* 76). This familiarity with Ludie is in large part due to Berenice's continued mention of him in conversation, and the topic of Berenice's first husband will re-emerge at the conclusion of the chapter. F. Jasmine then asks Berenice about T.T., Berenice's current beau, and why Berenice will not marry him. Berenice tells F. Jasmine that though T.T. is someone she "respect[s] and regard[s] highly," he doesn't "make me shiver" (*The Member of the Wedding* 77). F. Jasmine attempts to connect with Berenice's statement, telling her that thoughts about the wedding make her shiver.

F. Jasmine sees the "girls of fourteen and fifteen years old" walking across the backyard. These girls are members of the club from which the protagonist had previously been excluded. The narrator asserts:

> In the old days that summer she would have waited in the hope that they might call her and tell her she had been elected to the club—and only at the very last, when it was plain that they were only passing, she would have shouted in angry loudness that they were not to cut across her yard. But now she watched them quietly, without jealousy. (*The Member of the Wedding* 79)

This observation illustrates the extent to which the protagonist has shifted from an "unjoined" figure in Part One to a more connected character in Part Two. As was the case in Chapter One of Part Two, the protagonist is no longer jealous of other groups because she has constructed a sense of belonging. F. Jasmine, unlike Frankie in Part One, is a *member* of the wedding. Yet, it is this scene in Part One that prompts the protagonist to tell John Henry the reasons why she is not a part of the "older girls club", and this moment can thus be read as revisionist in scope. Moreover, it should be noted that this transformation occurs within the protagonist's mind, and, as the events of Part Three illustrate, this particular form of membership does not last.

The narrative moves from this observation to the "second

round of that last dinner" and it is past five o'clock (*The Member of the Wedding* 79). It is significant to note that the narrative, temporally speaking, still precedes the conclusion of Part One, which began at 5:45 in the afternoon. The conversation in this particular section between F. Jasmine, Berenice, and John Henry turns to God, and what they would do if they were God. John Henry asserts that, if he were God, he would create a world of sweet things to eat; Berenice envisions a realm with no war and where divisions between black and white did not exist; and F. Jasmine imagines a "world club with certificates and badges" and a place where "people could instantly change back and forth from boys to girls, whichever way they felt like and wanted" (*The Member of the Wedding* 80). Berenice argues with the protagonist on this last point, maintaining that such gender flexibility violates the laws of nature. Berenice then asks the protagonist to tell her about the experience she had in the alley, when F. Jasmine thought she saw Jarvis and Janice in the alley. After F. Jasmine recounts the story, Berenice tells her she understands the experience, and proceeds to tell F. Jasmine and John Henry about how, after Ludie's death, she began to see aspects of him in other men. For example, her second marriage to Jamie Beale was due to the fact that his thumb resembled Ludie's, and Berenice enumerates similar resemblance moments in her subsequent husbands. Berenice tells F. Jasmine that her other marriages represented vain attempts to recapture the feelings she had while married to Ludie, and cautions the protagonist against falling in with an idea like the wedding, for such thoughts lead to disappointment and disillusionment. It is significant to note that this conversation takes place at 5:45 in the evening, which temporally brings Part Two together with Part One. Thus, in Chapter Two, the two sections of the novel overlap, and Part Two represents a revisiting and a re-visioning of particular events in the previous section.

The conversation shifts its focus from love to names, and F. Jasmine asks Berenice why it is against the law to change one's name. Berenice maintains that changing one's name leads to confusion and that names, over time, accrete meanings that cannot be shed. This discussion has added significance given that the protagonist has changed names, and that these names represent different manifestations of her character. F. Jasmine pushes the conversation to a more philosophical plane; according to the protagonist:

> Doesn't it strike you as strange that I am I, and you are you? I am F. Jasmine Addams. You are Berenice Sadie Brown. And we can look at each other, and touch each other, and stay together year in and year out in the same room. Yet always I am I, and you are you. And I can't be anything else but me, and you can't ever be anything else but you. Have you ever though of that?
>
> *(The Member of the Wedding* 94)

F. Jasmine's assertion about the static nature of identity—the sense that one cannot be "anything else"—is interesting, given that the protagonist's name change from Part One to Part Two, which also encapsulates a shift in the way she conceptualizes herself vis-à-vis other individuals and groups. However, one can also read F. Jasmine's statements as reflective of the multi-faceted nature of identity, in which one can be both "Frankie" and "F. Jasmine." A person's essence, according to F. Jasmine, remains constant, even if the names change.

This conversation about identity and the separations that exist between F. Jasmine and Berenice dovetails into a larger discussion about segregation. Prior to this, however, is a scene in which F. Jasmine and Berenice silently hold on to one another. After F. Jasmine has thrown the knife and the ensuing chaos has died down, Berenice tells F. Jasmine to sit in her lap. According to the narrator, F. Jasmine

> had been breathing very fast, but after a minute her breath slowed down so that she breathed in time with Berenice; the two of them were close together as one body, and Berenice's stiffened hands were clasped around F. Jasmine's chest. *(The Member of the Wedding* 98)

This moment is reminiscent of the scene in the alley, in which F. Jasmine had spied two figures that simultaneously resembled her brother Jarvis and his fiancé and an ambiguous, singular figure. Berenice breaks the silence of the moment, saying to F. Jasmine that she understands "what [she] is driving at." Berenice continues, telling F. Jasmine that

> all of us somehow caught. We born this way or that way and we don't know why. But we caught anyhow ... I'm caught worse than you is.... Because I am black ... Because I am colored. Everybody is caught one way or another. But they done drawn completely extra bounds around all colored people. (*The Member of the Wedding* 98)

Berenice's statements illustrate the legacy of segregation and the realities of living in a world that is racialized and represents a sphere of oppression. The "otherness" that F. Jasmine feels in the first portion of the novel is thus echoed in Berenice, but there is a marked difference. Whereas F. Jasmine's sense of being an outsider is embedded in her lack of membership, Berenice's outsider status occurs as a result of her race, a fact that she will not "grow out of" nor is it something that can be changed by name or dress. F. Jasmine interjects, stating that one could also use the word "loose" instead of "caught," for the former connotes a sense of disconnectedness. This interjection reveals the protagonist's continued preoccupation with membership and belonging, even after the assumption of a more assertive and confident identity.

The conversation between Berenice and F. Jasmine shifts to war. The two embark on a discussion about the soldiers who are abroad fighting and dying. F. Jasmine maintains that there are "all these people and you don't know what joins them," and ponders what connects them. F. Jasmine then makes an observation that time passes and there is "no power on earth [that] could bring [time] back again" (*The Member of the Wedding* 100). Berenice does not answer F. Jasmine; instead, she begins to sing, and both F. Jasmine and John Henry accompany her. As they continue to sing, the three begin to cry in unison.

Chapter Two, Part Two concludes soon after this moment, in the evening. As the narrator notes, "Already the moths were at the window, flattening their wings against the screen, and the final kitchen afternoon was over at last" (*The Member of the Wedding* 101).

Chapter Three, Part Two begins with F. Jasmine's journey to Sugarville, the African American part of town. She is on her way to Big Mama's house (Berenice's mother) so that she can have her fortune read. John Henry follows F. Jasmine on her journey, and the two pass the jail and stare at the prisoners. F. Jasmine's reaction to the prisoners mirrors her reaction to the Freaks at the fair; the narrator reveals, "it seemed to her [F. Jasmine] that their eyes, like the long eyes of the Freaks at the fair, had called to her as though to say: We know you" (*The Member of the Wedding* 102). The two eventually leave the jail, and continue their journey to Big Mama's house. They arrive at the house at eight o' clock that evening, and F. Jasmine tells John Henry to stay outside.

F. Jasmine enters the home, and the narrator describes Big Mama as

> an old colored woman, shriveled and with bones like broomsticks; on the left side of her face and neck the skin was the color of tallow, so that part of her face was almost white and the rest copper-colored. The old Frankie used to think that Big Mama was slowly turning into a white person, but Berenice had said it was a skin disease that sometimes happened to colored people.
>
> (*The Member of the Wedding* 103)

This description is significant given the previous discussions about identity and the divisions between individuals that have occurred throughout the novel. Big Mama, as a figure, represents a blurring of multiple identities, and can metaphorically be read as a liminal figure who is both black and white. This blurring of identity coincides with both F. Jasmine's journey into adolescence, in which one is simultaneously a child and an adult. Just as the old Frankie "used to think that

Big Mama was slowly turning into a white person," the "new Frankie"—F. Jasmine—is slowly turning into an adult.

Big Mama, after putting on her glasses, proceeds to tell F. Jasmine's fortune. The protagonist tells her about her dream of opening a door, and Big Mama states that there will be a change in F. Jasmine's life. Big Mama furthers this announcement with the assertion that F. Jasmine will attend a wedding. Big Mama predicts that the protagonist will marry a "light-haired boy with blue eyes" and that she sees "a going and a coming back. A departure and a return" (*The Member of the Wedding* 105). F. Jasmine is troubled by the final part of Big Mama's prediction, for it does not reflect her decision to leave the town and join her brother and his bride. Big Mama, at the end of the reading, tells F. Jasmine that her "lucky number is six, although thirteen is sometimes lucky for you too" (*The Member of the Wedding* 106). This last point is important to note, for it foreshadows an event at the end of the novel. More specifically, F. Jasmine is thirteen years old when she befriends Mary Littlejohn; thus, thirteen is a lucky age for F. Jasmine— unlike twelve, which was marked by a lack of membership and a sense of being "unjoined," thirteen represents an age when the protagonist was once again "joined" to another.

Prior to the conclusion of the reading, Big Mama shouts at Honey, who is in the next room, and demands that he take his feet off the kitchen table. It is this moment of "clairvoyance" that solidifies F. Jasmine's faith in Big Mama's psychic ability and causes her to believe, in spite of her desire to do otherwise, in Big Mama's prediction. On her way out, F. Jasmine runs into Honey. The protagonist questions F. Jasmine about Big Mama's psychic capabilities, specifically citing the incident that involved him. It is Honey who tells her that Big Mama could see him in the next room, reflected on the door mirror, which partially undermines the authenticity of Big Mama's psychic abilities.

The narrative, and the protagonist, focuses its attention on Honey. According to Big Mama, Honey "was a boy God had not finished" and when she was younger, F. Jasmine imagined that Honey had half a body and only one foot. However, now that F. Jasmine is a little older, she realizes that Honey is, like her, searching for something, and that he is "incomplete". The protagonist feels a bit of a bond to Honey, and she attempts to give him advice about his life. Because he is light-skinned, F. Jasmine suggests that he go to Cuba, and maintains that he could "go there and change into a Cuban" (*The Member of the Wedding* 108). This suggestion coincides with F. Jasmine's belief that identities are fluid, and that one can shift from one to another. Honey dismisses F. Jasmine's suggestion, and disappears into an alley.

F. Jasmine and John Henry leave Big Mama's house and venture into town. John Henry tells F. Jasmine that they should head home, but F. Jasmine tells him the he should go on without her. F. Jasmine goes to the Blue Moon to meet the soldier. F. Jasmine meets the soldier, and the narrator observes that he

> was gay and his talk was sassy. But although she liked gay people and sassy talk, she could not think of any answers. It was again as though the soldier talked a kind of double-talk that, try as she would, she could not follow—yet it was not so much the actual remarks as the tone underneath she failed to understand.
>
> (*The Member of the Wedding* 110)

The above passage is reminiscent of the earlier scene with the soldier, and reminds the reader that F. Jasmine, though she enters the adult world embodied by the Blue Moon, is still naïve about sex and sexuality. Moreover, as the scene develops further, it becomes increasingly apparent to the reader that the protagonist has entered a situation that is beyond her immediate control.

The soldier brings two drinks to the table, and F. Jasmine, realizing that they are drinking alcohol, becomes disturbed by the thought that "it was a sin and against the law for people under eighteen to drink real liquor" and she pushes her glass away. She tries to, as in the previous meeting in the Blue Moon, make small talk with the solider, who seems disinterested. The protagonist then moves to the topic of the war, and the soldier refuses to talk about his experiences, preferring instead to continue making innuendos. As the narrator observes:

> To his joking remarks she could never find replies that fitted, although she tried. Like a nightmare pupil in a recital who has to play duet to a piece she does not know, F. Jasmine did her best to catch the tune and follow. But soon she broke down and grinned until her mouth felt wooden. The blue lights in the crowded room, the smoke and the noisy commotion, confused her also.
>
> (*The Member of the Wedding* 110)

The soldier asks F. Jasmine to go upstairs to his room, and though the protagonist is reluctant, she feels she cannot refuse. The two go to his room, and the protagonist perceives "a silence in the hotel room that warned and frightened her, a silence she noticed as soon as the door was closed" (*The Member of the Wedding* 111). This description, coupled with the protagonist's reaction, re-enforces the slippage that occurs in F. Jasmine's "adult identity"; put another way, though she would like to present herself as an adult, F. Jasmine is still a child and naïve. On another level, this scene again echoes the interaction the protagonist shared with Barney Mackean, which was sexual in scope.

When the soldier attempts to kiss F. Jasmine, she responds with an act of self-defense, biting his tongue and hitting him over the head with a glass pitcher. The soldier passes out, and the protagonist wonders if she has killed him. She runs out of the Blue Moon, which resembles the fair's "Crazy-House," and heads home. John Henry meets her on the corner of her street, and asks her why she is so upset. F. Jasmine tells him that she just "brained a crazy man," and when John Henry asks her to explain, the protagonist finds, "as she looked into those cold child eyes she knew that she could not explain" (*The Member of the Wedding* 113). F. Jasmine goes into the house and, seeing her father, asks him if it is possible to kill somebody with a glass pitcher. Her father interprets this as a non-serious, rhetorical question, telling her that he does not know because he has never hit anyone with a pitcher. He then asks F. Jasmine if she has committed such an act, and she replies that she will be so thankful when the wedding is over and that her new life will begin. Chapter Three, Part Two ends on this note, and the narrative has brought the reader to the latter part of the evening before the wedding.

As is the case in the previous two parts of *The Member of the Wedding*, **Part Three** begins with another name change, though it is important to note that it is the narrator, and not the protagonist, who refers to her as "Frances." In other words, whereas "F. Jasmine" was a self-selected name, one that the protagonist chose as her own, "Frances" is a name that the narrator uses and not the protagonist. This final name change marks both the end of the protagonist's journey, which includes structural and thematic elements. Structurally speaking, the protagonist's journey to the wedding is quickly rendered by the narrator. Few details are provided of the ceremony, and only a few sentences are devoted to the telling of the wedding. Thematically, as the events that follow the wedding illustrate, the protagonist's journey from childhood to adolescent is completed as the novel draws to a close.

The first paragraph of Part Three describes the four-hour trip to Winter Hill, the wedding, and Frances's attempt to call out to the couple as the wedding car drives away. The narrative then shifts to the trip home, and takes place on the bus. According to the narrator, "Frances wanted the whole world to die" (*The Member of the Wedding* 117) and the protagonist resents both John Henry and her father for not recognizing the significance of the wedding, which was supposed to signal the start of her new life. John Henry insightfully notes that "they [Jarvis and Janice] put old Frankie out of the wedding," and Frances's hope for inclusion has given way to an intense feeling of exclusion. Frances tries to find the reason why the wedding has been such a failure, and reflects on the failed card games from the summer. The narrator reveals:

> From the beginning the wedding had been queer like the card games in the kitchen he first week last June. In those bridge games they played and played for many days, but nobody ever drew a good hand.... finally Berenice suspicioned, saying: 'Less get busy and count these old cards' ... it turned out the jacks and the queens were missing. John Henry at last admitted that he had cut out the jacks and then the queens to keep them company and, after hiding the clipped scraps in the stove, had secretly taken the pictures home. (*The Member of the Wedding* 118)

Interestingly, John Henry pairs the jacks and the queens "to keep each other company," and it is the absence of these cards that causes the failure of the "card games in the kitchen." Though Frances, in this memory, finds the reason for the failure, another interpretation of the story can be made. More specifically, the failure of the came is attributed to the absence of male and female pairs, and one can argue that the "failure of the wedding" is due to the fact that Jarvis and Janice are paired, and there is no room for another person. Thus, the story of the cards provides another lens through which to consider the wedding, and this reading illustrates the extent to which Frances is unable to understand the adult relationships and marital dynamics.

Frances further reflects on the wedding, which "was all wrong, although she could not point out single faults." Those in attendance treat her like a child—for example, Mrs. Williams, one of the wedding guests, repeatedly asks Frances what grade she is in, and another guest urges her to go outside and play on the swing set. Both moments signals to the protagonist that she is viewed not as an adult but as a child. In addition, Frances partially attributes the failure of the wedding to the fact that she was not able to tell her brother and his bride her true feelings and intentions; according to the narrator, Frances

> stood in the corner of the bride's room, wanting to say: I love the two of you so much and you are the we of me.

Please take me with you from the wedding, for we belong together. (*The Member of the Wedding* 119)

It is this inability to speak, coupled with the reality that Frances never had an opportunity to be alone with the bride and groom, that the protagonist ultimately determines as reasons for the failure of the wedding, though the root causes behind each of these realities remains a mystery to the protagonist, who does not (and arguably, refuses to) understand that a marriage is a union between two, and not three, people.

Frances insists to all on the bus that her desire to get in the wedding car was a joke, and Berenice pretends to believe her. Berenice then changes the subject, and tells Frances that they should plan a dual bridge and costume party. Frances's disappointment, however, cannot be assuaged, and the two remain silent for the remainder of the trip back to the house. When the family returns to their home town, the sky is purple-gray, and it appears as if there is a large storm on the horizon. However, the rain never comes, and, as the narrator observes, "there was only a feeling of expectation in the air" (*The Member of the Wedding* 122). This "feeling of expectation" echoes Frances's previous anticipation about the wedding.

Once at home, Frances begins a letter to her father. According to the narrator, "They thought it was finished, but she would show them. The wedding had not included her, but she would still go into the world" (*The Member of the Wedding* 122). Though Frances does not know where she will go, she is certain that she will leave that night. She completes the letter, which informs her father of her plans to run away and tells him to not "capture" her. Before leaving the house, Frances takes her father's pistol. John Henry hears Frances leaving, and his cries awake Royal. Frances rushes out of the house and heads towards town. When she sees the train tracks, Frances contemplates hopping a freight train, but is dissuaded by the observation that the cars are parked on the tracks and not connected to any engines. Frances then moves to an alley behind Finney's Place and sets her suitcase down. Frances, with her father's pistol still in her left hand, remembers that she threatened to commit suicide if her brother and his bride did not take her away with them. Frances thinks about fulfilling this threat, but elects instead to put the gun in her suitcase.

While in the alley, Frances "was scared ... and felt her mind splintered." She remembers that it was in this alley that Lon Baker was murdered, and she feels isolated and disconnected. She contemplates possible travel companions, including Honey Brown and the organ grinder and his pet monkey, but her thoughts are interrupted by the noise of a cat in the alley. Frances initially thinks that this is Charles, her missing cat, but soon acknowledges that it is not. Frances then turns her mental attention to Big Mama, realizing that her prediction has come true, and considers visiting her house and seeking more advice.

Frances, still in the alley, spots two people on the opposite sidewalk, and, according to the narrator:

> a feeling like a sudden flame sprang up in side her, and for less than a second it seemed that her brother and the bride had come for her and were now *there*. But the feeling blew out instantly and she was just watching a stranger couple passing down the street. There was a hollow in her chest, but at the bottom of this emptiness a heavy weight pressed down and bruised her stomach, so that she felt sick. (*The Member of the Wedding* 126)

It is significant to note both the setting and the scope of the above passage. It was, after all, in the same alley that Frances sees the two boys who resemble her brother and his fiancé, and it is this vision that causes Frances such happiness in Part Two. However, this second vision in the alley occurs after the wedding, and the outcome is markedly different. This second vision is much more ephemeral, as if the experience of the wedding has made Frances a less naïve figure, a person who cannot extend the fantasy of her brother and his bride for more "then a second." On another level, this passage reveals the extent of Frances's disillusionment. The protagonist imagines that the wedding will solve her lack of connectedness in the world, though in actuality the exact opposite has occurred.

This section of Part Three, after all, focuses its narratival attention on the solo journey Frances takes through town—she is unaccompanied and talks to no one. Thus, instead of connection, Frances now lives, in this moment, in isolation.

After spending much time in the alley, Frances eventually leaves, and her thoughts turn to the solider. She wonders if she should go to the Blue Moon and find out if she has killed the solider before leaving town. She then recalls Big Mama's prediction that she will marry a "light-haired man with blue eyes," and contemplates marrying the soldier. She heads over to the Blue Moon, and she realizes, while standing in front of the building, that

> She was no longer thinking of the soldier; the discovery of the moment before had scattered him from her mind. There was only knowing before that she must find somebody, and anybody, that she could join to go away. For now she admitted she was too scared to go into the world alone. (*The Member of the Wedding* 127)

Thus, Frances realizes, in this moment, that she is "too scared to go into the world alone" and that she needs a companion. The narrative has come full circle—as was the case in Part One, the protagonist in Part Three is scared of being alone, yet she also admits, to herself, that this is the cause of her fear. This admission signals the growth of the protagonist—though alone, she is considerably more self-aware.

While Frances is at the Blue Moon, she is intercepted by "the Law"—her father had called the police station to report her disappearance. The police officer waits with her at the Blue Moon, and Royal eventually picks her up from the bar. The narrative shifts from this scene into the future, and the narrator informs the reader that "Frances was never once to speak about the wedding. Weathers had turned and it was another season. There were the changes and Frances was now thirteen" (*The Member of the Wedding* 129). The final pages of the novel are characterized by a factual and speedy narrative which quickly takes the reader to its conclusion. In the time after the wedding, Frances has befriended Mary Littlejohn, who is two years older than Frances, and the two of them have plans to travel the world. They attend the town fair, but avoid the House of Freaks. Royal decides to relocate the family to Aunt Pet and Uncle Ustace's house in the suburbs. Honey, while under the influence of marijuana, robs a store and is now spending sentence in jail. And, John Henry gets meningitis, which causes him to go blind, and he dies in ten days as a result of his illness. The kitchen has been repainted and redecorated, and Berenice has given her notice, deciding to marry T.T. Williams. Thus, the kitchen scene that so dominated the narrative has effectively become, like the protagonist's personas and her preoccupation with the wedding, a thing of the past.

The novel concludes with the news that the family has received a letter from Jarvis, who is now in Luxembourg. Frances comments that Luxembourg is "a lovely name." She then tells Berenice that "we will most likely pass through Luxembourg when we go around the world together" (*The Member of the Wedding* 132). It is significant that, in this final moment, Frances uses "we," referring to herself and Mary Littlejohn, for it signals to the reader that she has finally found a connection and, unlike the opening pages of the novel, she is "joined" and a "member." The novel ends with the ringing of the doorbell, which is described by the narrator as "an instant shock of happiness" (*The Member of the Wedding* 132).

Notes

1. Quote taken from Judith Giblin James's *Wunderkind: The Reputation of Carson McCullers, 1940–1990*, p. 10.

2. From Richard M. Cook's *Carson McCullers* (New York: Unagar Publishing Co., 1975. p. 13). Quoted from a letter to Reeves that appeared in Oliver Evans, *The Ballad of Carson McCullers*, p. 100.

3. This detail about Frankie's mother is given in Part Two, Chapter 1.

Works Cited

McCullers, Carson. *The Member of the Wedding*. Boston: Houghton Mifflin Company, 1946.

Critical Views

This is Carson McCullers's third book; and we have now, I should think, sufficient evidence for remarking that, while there are quite a few writers who unfortunately resemble her, she fortunately resembles nobody else. She is unique.

The Member of the Wedding is, more or less, the story of four days in the life of Frankie Addams: how she had become "an unjoined person who hung around in doorways"; how the thought of her brother's approaching wedding gave her a sense of sharing in the world again; how she went out into the town to test this new feeling with rather violent consequences; how she talked around and around the subject of the wedding when she was at home; how the wedding, eventually, was a ghastly failure for her; and how Frankie grew up.

But to write about *The Member of the Wedding* in this way is like writing about a tent pole and forgetting to describe the tent.

But it would be extremely difficult and quite unnecessary to make an adequate précis of this (as the publishers and perhaps the author like to label it) novella. It is not just a study of adolescence. Frankie Addams, it is true, conforms to a possible pattern of behavior. She does nothing which a twelve-year-old girl might not do. Yet the further you read into *The Member of the Wedding* the more you realize, it seems to me, that Frankie is merely the projection of a problem that has nothing much to do with adolescence.

The three chief characters are Frankie herself, her six-and-a-half-year-old cousin John Henry, and the thirty-eight-year-old, one-eyed cook Berenice. At times these three personages behave as if, indeed, one was twelve, one six and a half, and one thirty-eight; but generally they are beings of no special age, discoursing in what appears to be a dream or trance. Their problem is elementary, unanswerable, and common to all age levels. Here is the crux of it:

"I know, but what is it all about? People loose and at the same time caught. Caught and loose. All these people and you don't know what joins them up. There's bound to be some sort of reason and connection. Yet somehow I can't seem to name it. I don't know."

"If you did you would be God," said Berenice. "Didn't you know that?"

In other words, the problem which obsesses them is human loneliness: the basic problem which Virginia Woolf, after years of investigation, could only state in terms of "here is one room, there another." Miss McCullers states it in its most undifferentiated form; places it in this light and in that; looks at it savagely, gleefully, tenderly; seems almost to taste it and to roll it round her tongue; but never attempts to find an answer.

Indeed, what makes this story so unusual is the fact that most of it takes place through the medium of desultory conversations between three really weird people sitting in an even weirder kitchen. Nothing or almost nothing occurs here, and yet every page is filled with a sense of something having happened, happening, and about to happen. This in itself is a considerable technical feat; and, beyond that, there is magic in it.

The words used above—"dream," "trance," "loneliness," "weird," "magic"—are such as are generally applied to work which has severe limitations. I would be the last to deny that Miss McCullers has hers. It must be obvious to everyone who has read her books that her art excludes many important things with which the artist today is rightly preoccupied. It is an exclusive arc, not out of choice but out of necessity: not because it does not wish to include but because it cannot.

She is a suggestive rather than an eloquent writer, and often seems to present us less with a meaning than with a hint. And yet the lines of her work are clear and firm. I do not know how this is done; but my ignorance will not deter me from attempting to provide an explanation.

Though she has an acute observation, she does not use it to make rounded people. Her characters invariably remind one of faces one *may have* seen, in a dream perhaps, in a tabloid newspaper possibly, or out of a train window. Their clothes, their gestures, their conversations are selected with an admirable eye and ear to verisimilitude; but the actual inhabitants of these clothes, gestures, and conversations are not themselves quite human. In fact, this book seems more and more to insist that it is, as it were, a monologue furnished with figures.

For Carson McCullers's work has always seemed to me to be a form of self-dramatization. It is true that this can be said of most immature fiction. But Miss McCullers is both a mature and fine writer. She does not dramatize herself in the sense that she is merely autobiographical; but she does dramatize herself in the sense that she seems to invest the various sides of her personality with attributes skilfully collected from the outside world.

From this point of view, *The Member of the Wedding* is a masquerade; but a serious, profound, and poetic masquerade in which the Unconscious (or the Subconscious or whatever you wish to call the subliminal personality) expresses itself, now through the voice of Frankie Addams, now through that of John Henry, now through that of Berenice Sadie Brown. The other characters, who certainly belong to the real world, hover round the edge of this extraordinary monologue, with one foot in it and one out; behaving with none of the awkwardness which you might expect from them in such circumstances, but adding richness to the story and relating it to more normal fiction.

I suppose that I have not yet made it clear that this is, to my mind, a marvelous piece of writing. Not merely does it sustain the interest all the way through, but it does so under circumstances which demand the utmost delicacy and balance from the author.

The book avoids what T.E. Lawrence called "the kindergarten of the imagination" on the one hand; on the other hand, it never becomes a mere sequence of neurotic images. It steers a wonderful middle course between these two morasses. It is a work which reveals a strong, courageous, and independent imagination. There are other writers in the contemporary field who are of more importance than Carson McCullers. Of her it should be sufficient to say, once again, that she is unique.

Robert S. Phillips on the Gothic Elements

Leslie Fiedler has stated in *An End to Innocence* that "images of childhood and adolescence haunt our greatest works as an unintended symbolic confession of the inadequacy we sense but cannot remedy." *The Member of the Wedding* (1946) is a very intentional use of the adolescent as symbol for that sense of inadequacy and helplessness. The novel's title refers to Frankie Addams, a sensitive and fearful child whose thirteenth summer is the subject of the novel. The cast of characters is very small—Frankie primarily associates with only two other people—and the book is a study of her loneliness and isolation. Frankie's fears are the fears of all human beings, and the last name of Addams indicates her archetypal function in her initiation into worldly knowledge. The self-chosen nickname of Frankie (like the name Mick Kelly) is a feeble effort on the part of the adolescent to assert her individuality in a patriarchal culture, as is the crew cut which makes her a neuter being.

The summer during which the novel's action occurs is described as "the summer of fear," and Frankie is plagued by many nightmares and terrible visions. It is for this reason that the novel can be called Gothic, and not because there is "a female homosexual romance between the boy-girl Frankie and a Negro cook" as Fiedler so glibly conjectures. One dream which frightens Frankie is of a beckoning door which slowly begins to open and draw her in. What lies beyond that door—maturity, truth, knowledge—is a mystery to her, and she is frightened by the unknown. Frankie is afraid of her own growth. Having grown four inches in the past year, she towers above her classmates and is fearful that she will become "a lady who is over nine feet high. She would be a Freak." Frankie visits the carnival's Freak House, and has been terrified by the knowing eyes of the grotesques she sees there: "it seemed to her they had looked at her in a secret way and tried to connect their eyes with hers, as though to say: We know you." Frankie feels the grotesques have recognized her own freakish and guilt-ridden soul.

The Freak House is not the only place that frightens the girl: "the jail had scared and haunted her that spring and summer." She also feels the ghastly looking prisoners "know her" for what she is—and that she too is trapped, though she is free to move about and they are not. The very existence of the jail house haunts her: "the criminals were caged in stone cells with iron bars before the windows, and though they might beat on the stone walls or wrench at the iron bars, they could never get out." Frankie imagines herself so trapped, and her confidante, Berenice Sadie Brown, reveals to her that it is the human predicament.

A third house she visits which terrifies her is the residence of Big Mama, an old fortune-telling Negress said to possess supernatural powers. Though Frankie fears her she turns to Big Mama's powers in her search for answers to the ultimate question of human suffering and death, the problem of evil. But Frankie is not satisfied with the answers Big Mama gives her, and she is left with her feeling of "the sense of something terribly gone wrong."

Running away from one frightening scene only to encounter another, Frankie is the Gothic heroine encountering the chambers of horrors. In the course of the summer she is haunted by three gruesome deaths of acquaintances. These deaths are described by Mrs. McCullers in very graphic terms, the verbal intensity matching the strong impressions made upon Frankie's mind. The first of these is the unmotivated murder of the Negro boy, Lon Baker, in the alley directly behind her father's jewelry store:

On an April afternoon his throat was slashed with a razor blade, and all the alley people disappeared in back doorways, and later it was said his cut throat opened like a crazy shivering mouth that spoke ghost words into the April sun.

The silent flapping mouth of Lon's throat parallels Frankie's own inarticulate attempts at communication.

The death of her Uncle Charles is more immediate to Frankie, and his ghastly passing pricks her awareness of mortality and her own insignificance in the cosmos. She fears death:

> He lay in the bed, shrunken and brown and very old. Then his voice failed and when he tried to talk, it was as though his throat had filled with glue, and they could not understand the words. He looked like an old man carved in brown wood and covered with a sheet. Only his eyes had moved, and they were like blue jelly, and she had felt they might come out from the sockets and roll like blue wet jelly down his stiff face. She had stood in the doorway staring at him—then tiptoed away, afraid.

Again Frankie is aghast not only because of the pain involved in dying, but also because of the hopeless inability of the dying to communicate to the living.

The greatest shock however comes with the death of John Henry, her only young friend. Sickly and frail, John Henry in his confinement had become associated in Frankie's mind with her own isolation. The two of them seemed to share the same condition as recluses and even outcasts. With the loss of this rapport, Frankie finally feels any meaning to her life has vanished. All that remains is the spirit of John Henry which seems to visit her.

Sitting in the kitchen she "felt his presence there, solemn and hovery and ghost-gray." Time and again she is to recall his torturous death:

> John Henry had been screaming for three days and his eyeballs were walled up in a corner, stuck and blind. He lay there finally with his head drawn back in a buckled way, and he had lost the strength to scream. He died the Tuesday after the Fair was gone.

This last statement reveals much of what Frankie has had to learn. After the fair—the brief pleasantries of life—comes the blackness of death. But *The Member of the Wedding* is more than a novel of one girl's initiation; it is impossible to read the account of John Henry's death and still regard the work as a charming account of adolescence as many critics have done. In its cataloguing of death scenes the novel plays upon the reader's fear of death and the dead, a characteristic theme of Gothic novels.

The story's action primarily occurs in a setting which is ominous and depressing to the heroine. There is no dank dungeon in the novel—but the kitchen of the Addams home is a place of confinement and dread for Frankie. Spurned by the other girls because of her unusual size, Frankie finds herself continually sitting in the dark kitchen whose very walls she hates. The kitchen is Frankie's private hell, "a sad and ugly room," and Frankie often feels she will go berserk if she has to remain there any longer. Indeed the kitchen is like "a room in the crazy-house," because John Henry has covered the walls with queer and childish drawings which run together in confusion: "The walls of the kitchen bothered Frankie—the queer drawings of Christmas trees, airplanes, freak soldiers, flowers." Such varied drawings make the walls a projection of the world itself, a microcosm of the macrocosm. Frankie in her confinement seems to sense this, staring at the walls and commenting that "the world is certainly a small place." Life is hell for the adolescent Frankie; she feels there is no escape from her fate, and she hates her environment, thinking she "lived in the ugliest house in town," viewing the sunshine as "the bars of a bright, strange jail." Such imagery clearly reveals the author deliberately giving us another trapped, suffering and helpless female within a Gothic framework, every bit as anguished as Alison Langdon of *Reflections in a Golden Eye*, her most overtly Gothic novel.

Shortly after the publication of *Reflections in a Golden Eye* in 1941, Carson McCullers began writing *The Member of the Wedding*. She finished the book five years later in 1946, having interrupted work on it in 1943 for a short period to write the novella *The Ballad of the Sad Café*. The general area of experience described in *The Member of the Wedding*, that of an adolescent girl growing up in a small Southern town, was, of course, one that McCullers was intimately familiar with and one she had already treated in her description of Mick Kelley in *The Heart Is a Lonely Hunter*. It was evidently a subject to which she was willing to dedicate a great deal of time and hard work. In a letter written to Reeves McCullers in 1945 quoted previously she wrote: "It's [*The Member of the Wedding*] one of those works that the least slip can ruin. Some parts I have worked over and over as many as twenty times.... It must be beautifully done. For like a poem there is not much excuse for it otherwise."[1]

Once completed, *The Member of the Wedding* did full justice to her efforts. Its plot is clear and perfectly controlled; its setting, though less detailed, is as definite and evocative of the mood and temper of the small town in the South as is that in *The Heart Is a Lonely Hunter*. And its characters are as fully drawn as any she created. In "The Flowering Dream" McCullers, referring to her writing of *The Member of the Wedding*, wrote: "To understand a work, it is important for the artist to be emotionally right on dead center; to see, to know, to experience the things he is writing about." Carson McCullers knew what she was writing about in this novel in the way Mark Twain knew what he was about in *The Adventures of Huckleberry Finn* and J.D. Salinger knew what he was about in *The Catcher in the Rye*. As a portrait embodying the spirit and detail of adolescence, Carson McCullers's Frankie Addams is an achievement comparable to Twain's Huck Finn and Salinger's Holden Caulfield.

The Member of the Wedding tells the story of Frankie Addams's struggle to become a member arid an adult during the final days of "that green and crazy summer when Frankie was twelve years old." Frankie Addams, who "belonged to no group and was a member of nothing in the world," is another of McCullers's isolated people, except that instead of being isolated because of some physical or sexual defect that would have made her a grotesque, Frankie is isolated by her age. No longer a child and not yet an adult, she is caught in a stage in which everything has become disconnected and she has become "an unjoined person who hung around in doorways and ... was afraid."

The Member of the Wedding is a novel about the loneliness, the uncertainties of identity, and the plain foolishness, associated with adolescence. Frankie's unhappiness in her unjoined state is pathetic and often humorous. It could not be called tragic, because her situation by its very nature is an impermanent one. Her fate unlike Singer's, Copeland's, and Penderton's, remains open. Yet Frankie's plight during the bad summer months bears an important similarity to that of McCullers's adult grotesques, in that Frankie, like them, is being forced into an awareness of her own separateness, her own isolated self. And in McCullers's world such awareness is all but unbearable. What forces this terrible knowledge on Frankie is the very fact of her evolving maturity. As McCullers in a later essay entitled "Loneliness ... An American Malady" has written, maturity is a conscious and continuing process, during which the individual comes to a recognition of self and then strives to merge that self into a larger identity:

> Consciousness of self is the first abstract problem that the human being solves. Indeed, it is this self-consciousness that removes us from lower animals. This primitive grasp of identity develops with constantly shifting emphasis through all our years. Perhaps maturity is simply the history of those mutations that reveal to the individual the relation between himself and the world in which he finds himself.

After the first establishment of identity there comes the imperative need to lose this new-found sense of separateness and to belong to something larger and more powerful than the weak, lonely self....

In *The Member of the Wedding* the lonely 12-year-old girl, Frankie Addams, articulates this universal need: "The trouble with me is that for a long time I have just been an I person. All people belong to a *We* except me. Not to belong to a *We* makes you too lonesome."

(...)

Frankie's experiences throughout the summer might be described as a teenage version of existential dread—terribly serious to Frankie but slightly absurd to everyone else. Berenice refers to her moods and behavior as "foolishness," "just foolishness." Sometimes Frankie would hear a noise at night or see a light in the distance and be suddenly overwhelmed by tension and fear: "These things made her suddenly wonder who she was, and what she was going to be in the world and why she was standing at that minute seeing a light or listening or staring up into the sky: alone." Yet the next minute she would "go home, put a coal scuttle on her head, like a crazy person's hat, and walk around the kitchen table." Or she would exclaim loudly, violently and melodramatically against herself and the whole world: "I just wish I could tear down the whole town." "I am sick unto death." "I feel exactly like somebody has peeled all the skin off me. I wish I had some good cold chocolate ice-cream."

McCullers has written in her essay "The Vision Shared" that one thing she was trying to do in *The Member of the Wedding* was write a "lyric tragicomedy in which the funniness and the grief coexist in the same line." She manages to keep the grief and the funniness of Frankie's situation together by never letting us forget that Frankie's fears, for all their terrible, consuming indefiniteness are adolescent fears and have their source in Frankie's adolescent misunderstanding and inexperience.

Thus when Frankie steals the knife from Sears and Roebuck, she concludes axiomatically that she is a criminal and a no-good. Similarly when Frankie begins to worry about her recent growth—she has grown four inches in the last year—she assumes that she is destined to be a freak. She sees it as a matter of mere mathematics. This "was one fear that could be figured in arithmetic with paper and a pencil at the table." She calculates how much she has grown in the past year and projects that by the time she has her complete growth "according to mathematics and unless she could somehow stop herself, she would grow to be over nine feet tall. And what would be a lady who is over nine feet high? She would be a Freak." She is more certain of becoming a freak when she remembers her visit to the freak show at the fair a year ago. For "it seemed to her that they [the freaks] had looked at her in a secret way and tried to connect their eyes with hers, as though to say: we know you."

(...)

Recent criticism of *The Member of the Wedding* has alternated between enthusiasm for McCullers's sensitive portrayal of an adolescent experience, which in Lawrence Graver's words, is "available to everyone,"[6] and universal in its implications about love and loneliness, and disappointment with McCullers for retreating into a childish, solipsistic world removed from the social and political realities confronted in *The Heart Is a Lonely Hunter*. Chester Eisinger originally made this charge in 1963 when he wrote that McCullers had taken up no new themes in *The Member of the Wedding* and had, in fact, restricted her interests by focusing "on the child's self-centered world in which the macrocosm plays no part."[7] More recently Alfred Kazin has leveled the same accusation to the effect that the book shows a retreat from matters of serious social significance to juvenile entertainment. "*The Member of the Wedding* ... turns the *Huckleberry Finn* of her first novel into the children's literature of Tom Sawyer."[8] The charge is a serious one. Though McCullers does, in fact, take up a new theme in *The*

Member of the Wedding, namely, the role of time in human affairs, she does not pursue her interests in the social, racial, and political problems that were important to her in her first novel. And because she demonstrated such an acute sensitivity and humane grasp of these larger social issues in *The Heart Is a Lonely Hunter*, we do feel the loss in the later novel.

On the other hand, McCullers was trying to write a very different kind of novel in *The Member of the Wedding*. Like *The Heart Is a Lonely Hunter*, its concern is with human isolation and man's struggle to overcome it. But instead of portraying this struggle in the public arena where individual perversity and misunderstanding between people result in social injustice, political activism, and crime, McCullers in this work dramatizes the more personal, private problems arising out of isolation by examining its effect on the consciousness of a single individual, Frankie Addams. *The Member of the Wedding* is in this sense an "inward" novel, a term McCullers once used to describe the Broadway play made from the book. And its achievement lies in McCullers's success at recreating the feelings of its protagonist through a simple plot and a highly evocative, poetic style. Instead of portraying the various social forces at work within Frankie's surroundings, McCullers has personalized, or internalized, them, turning the details of Frankie's world into manifestations of her complex, shifting, and rather diffuse emotions. The world Frankie sees and hears and imagines—the kitchen, "silent and crazy and sad," the earth "enormous and still and flat"—is not the outside political, racial world, but McCullers's description of Frankie herself and the way she feels. And the language used to describe this world—the afternoon, dense and solid like the center of Berenice's cake that had failed—is a richly metaphoric language used to suggest the peculiar preoccupations and limits of Frankie's imagination. It is undoubtedly this method of making the detail and language of the novel both reveal and conform to the personality and moods of its heroine that prompted McCullers to remark that *The Member of the Wedding* "is one of those works that the least slip can ruin." The inwardness of the novel means she must tell Frankie's story from within Frankie's world. She cannot afford to take up pressing social issues outside Frankie's ken. To do so would violate the method and the theme of the novel. It would not conform to the novel's poetry, and *The Member of the Wedding*, as McCullers has written, must be "like a poem, there's not much excuse for it otherwise."[9]

Notes

1. Quoted in Oliver Evans, *The Ballad of Carson McCullers* (New York: Coward-McCann, Inc., 1966), p. 100.

6. Lawrence Graver, *Carson McCullers*, p. 33.

7. Chester E. Eisinger, *Fiction of the Forties* (Chicago: The University of Chicago Press, Phoenix Books, 1963), pp. 255–256.

8. Alfred Kazin, *Bright Book of Life: American Novelists and Story Tellers from Hemingway to Mailer* (Boston: Little, Brown and Co., An Atlantic Monthly Press Book, 1973), p. 53.

9. Quoted in Oliver Evans, *The Ballad of Carson McCullers*, p. 100.

MARGARET B. MCDOWELL ON THE RELATIONSHIP BETWEEN BERENICE AND FRANKIE

If this novella presented only the conflicts within the life of Frankie and their partial resolution as she matures through a crisis, McCullers would undoubtedly have made use of more conventional methods to portray the "rites of passage" from childhood to adult society. She would still have achieved a work of significant insight into the psyche of the female early adolescent. The unusual achievement of this book, however, resides in McCullers' depiction of Frankie, though in many ways a typical adolescent, as a freak and a prisoner. The aesthetic distinction of the book derives even more from McCullers' skilled refraction of Frankie's conflicts against those of Berenice Sadie Brown.[5] The "precision and balance" which McCullers continually sought in writing this novella lie most notably in her skilled revelation of Berenice and Frankie through their almost continuous contact with each other. (In the play this effect is even more concentrated, because all of the scenes take place in the kitchen or adjoining yard. The Blue Moon scenes and the wedding—which occurs in the Addams's living room—are reported to Berenice as events which take place offstage.) The problems and responses of Frankie, echoed in those of the older Berenice, achieve a universal significance, because they are seen to be the preoccupations and the aspirations of another generation and another race.

Though Frankie and Berenice experience similar fears and hopes, they often become extreme antagonists. Their differences are as great as their similarities. In the relationships existing between the two women, McCullers can dramatize most effectively the conflicts between black and white, between old and young, and even between mother and daughter. Berenice's hostility is barely smothered in her patronizing remarks to Frankie: "I believe the sun has fried your brains" (600), or "You jealous.... Go and behold yourself in the mirror. I can see from the color in your eye" (600). When Frankie, disgusted with her gangling appearance, cries, "I just wish I would die," Berenice, with no tenderness, replies, "Well, die then" (621). Frankie storms away from her and verbally, in turn, abuses John Henry. Repeatedly, Berenice mocks Frankie when she loses control and rages at herself and the whole world. Such condescension and harshness often succeed in getting Frankie back to reality and behaving sensibly: "I intend to sit by myself and think over everything for a while!" (620) she says, after one very stormy situation. At other times, Berenice's taunts arouse in Frankie more bitterness and violence than they curb. In one instance, Frankie's response is to throw a knife so fast across the kitchen that it embeds itself in a door, and in another scene, she threatens, "Some day you going to look down and find that big fat tongue of yours pulled out by the roots and laying there before you on the table" (637). Berenice's behavior toward Frankie is characterized as much by her shouting, "Devil!" at Frankie as by her inviting Frankie to climb into her lap when she feels most afraid and alone.

McCullers' "precision and balance" lie also in this skilled fusion of opposing emotions, like love and anger, which characterize the relationship throughout the book between Frankie and Berenice and, to a lesser degree, that between Frankie and her father and that between Frankie and John Henry. Ethel Waters may have brought Berenice in the stage play and motion picture too close to the "mammy" stereotype, for McCullers' conception of her is much more complex. Berenice energetically responds to the turmoil in Frankie; always strongly and sometimes negatively. Frankie, in turn, can fight more intensely the authority characterizing for her the adult world when it is represented in a servant than in a parent.

McCullers goes beyond a presentation of the antagonism between generations and beyond the two individuals to show the violent and complex conflicts both women experience within themselves. McCullers relates the war within Frankie's psyche to the inward war that Berenice experiences when she finally lets Ludie die, as she decides to marry a far different man, T.T. Williams, for his own goodness. When Frankie and Berenice talk philosophically and with deep emotion, one sometimes hears dynamic dialogue as the women clash with each other and alternately reveal the anger and the tenderness they feel for each other. More often, however, one hears a rising antiphony in which one woman speaks, the other speaks in a contrasting tone, and finally the two join to achieve unified utterance, sometimes revealing a deep accord; sometimes a frustrating inability to communicate. In these antiphonal scenes, the two women do not necessarily speak to each other or to John Henry. Rather each speaks aloud to herself or to a vaguely conceived and undefined audience, which may or may not include the other two people present.

A sophisticated curiosity and an acute speculativeness mark Frankie's thoughtful words, and it is partly her tragedy that she fails to sustain her originality of mind and lapses in the last pages into banal acceptance of convention. At times, she and Berenice share a surprising wisdom in their conversation; at other times, Berenice marvels at Frankie's foolishness. At times, she perceptively understands the child's mind. Frankie, who longs to be understood, paradoxically rages whenever the older woman understands her too well. Berenice can also deflect too easily, with her common sense and her jealousy of Frankie's youth, the girl's untamed aspirations.

When Berenice and Frankie talk about the mysteries of individuality and the vastness of the universe, they become so intent on sharing the other's insight that they feel in awe of each other when they recognize their closeness. Berenice is strongly moved, for example, when Frankie hesitantly divulges the momentary vision she had downtown that morning, the day before the wedding: Jarvis and Janice were in Winter Hill preparing for the wedding, but Frankie saw them, for a few seconds, walking beside her. Berenice is overwhelmed by Frankie's revelation, because she has herself at times had a glimpse of her dead first husband, Ludie, walking beside her. She had thought that she was the only human being in the world to have such a supernatural experience.

If one central theme of the book is Frankie's need to achieve a sense of identity with others, this sharing of a supernatural experience marks the closest approach to the imaginative conjoining of Frankie and Berenice. It is followed, in fact, by a kind of communion ceremony. Frankie reaches over and takes one of Berenice's cigarettes. Berenice allows her to do so; for the first time, Frankie sits smoking with an adult. Frankie and Berenice are at several other times remarkably congruent in their preoccupations and insights, considering their antagonism and the fact that one lives in anticipation while the other lives in memory. While Frankie waits impatiently to move into adulthood, Berenice longs to return to the past—the snowy winters in Cincinnati before her first husband, Ludie, died. In the hot South, she has three times married men who fleetingly reminded her of Ludie. (One wore Ludie's overcoat, which she had sold to pay his funeral expenses; another merely had a scarred thumb which looked like Ludie's.) Whenever Berenice recounts for John Henry and Frankie the romantic saga that begins with her meeting Ludie at sunset near a filling station and reaches its height with her entertaining twenty-eight people at a fish fry, sewing on a new machine, getting a fox fur for Christmas, and walking in snow in Cincinnati, the children see her transformed into a queen, radiantly unrolling her life for them like a splendid bolt of gold cloth.

Note

5. Leslie Fiedler suggests this novel is a "homosexual romance" between Berenice and Frankie (*An End to Innocence: Essays on Culture and Politics* [Boston, 1955], p. 202). Frankie's immaturity and sexual naiveté, as well as Berenice's strong heterosexual interests, would argue against the plausibility of such interpretation.

LOUISE WESTLING ON THE TOMBOY FIGURE AND THE MOTIF OF "UNFINISHED-NESS"

With the character of Frankie Addams we return to the type of the ambitious tomboy on the brink of puberty, baffled by incomprehensible changes in her life. This time the heroine's ambitions are literary rather than musical; Frankie Addams writes plays and dreams of becoming a great poet. Her ambitions are not blighted as Mick's are, but it could be argued that Frankie's attitude toward writing has changed significantly by the end of the novel. However, the focus of McCullers's attention in this book is not on the protagonist's dreams of fame but rather on the psychological trauma she suffers when required to accept her femininity. By the end of the novel she has passed from childhood into adolescence with an acceptance of the facts of adult sex. In the process of attaining her new status, she follows the same general pattern as Mick Kelly. We meet her as a twelve-year-old tomboy with a boy's name and haircut, who wears shorts and a B.V.D. undershirt. She is an expert knife-thrower and has the toughest bare feet in town. Toward the middle of the story, she transforms herself by changing her name to F. Jasmine and putting on a pink organdy dress, lipstick, and Sweet Serenade perfume. She has made herself into a romantic caricature of a female, much as Mick Kelly did for her prom party. As she parades around town in her finery, F. Jasmine meets a soldier who takes her for much older than she is, and with him she has her first adult sexual encounter. This dismaying experience forces her to admit to what men and women do together. Her last illusions are shattered when her brother and his bride refuse to let her go along on their honeymoon. At the end of the book we find her completely changed into a giddy teenager, having accepted her femininity and her real name, Frances.

Before this transformation can occur, however, Frankie suffers agonies of loneliness, feelings of entrapment, and fears of freakishness which hover around her in the shapes of the prodigies she has seen at the fair. There are several kinds of freaks—which Frankie and her little cousin John Henry West visit at the Chattahoochee Exposition. She is afraid of all of them, but Ellen Moers is right to single out the hermaphrodite as she most important, for it is the quintessential symbol of Frankie's danger. Images of sexual ambivalence are carefully cultivated throughout the novel in the Negro transvestite Lily Mae Jenkins, the Utopias invented by Frankie and John Henry where one could change sex at will or be half male and half female, and John Henry's interest in dolls and dressing in women's clothes. Always such hermaphroditic or androgynous references are placed in a negative frame, for the novel's entire movement is towards Frankie's ultimate submission to the inexorable demand that she accept her sex as female. Just after telling Frankie about Lily Mae Jenkins, wise old Berenice urges her to start looking for beaus and acting feminine. "Now you belong to change from being so rough and greedy and big. You ought to fix yourself up nice in your dresses. And speak sweetly and act sly."[20] Berenice also refuses to countenance sexual transformation in the Utopian dreams she and Frankie and John Henry spin on summer afternoons. Children may play at exchanging sex roles, but adults may not, unless they are to be regarded as grotesques fit only for sideshow displays.

This truth begins to force itself upon Frankie Addams in the "green and crazy summer" of her twelfth year. "Frankie had become an unjoined person who hung around in doorways, and she was afraid." McCullers emphasizes the element of fear so rhythmically that the novel's opening pages swim in a fevered, hallucinatory atmosphere. The central setting is the sad and ugly kitchen, like the room of a crazy house, its walls covered with John Henry's freakish drawings. Here a vague terror squeezes Frankie's heart. And here she, Berenice, and John Henry constitute a strange family or private world cut off from any other. The real doorway where Frankie lingers in baffled fright is the passage between childhood and the clearly defined sexual world of grown-ups which she must enter, for almost all of the specific sources of her anxiety turn out to be sexual. The older girls who have shut her out of their club are preoccupied with boys and gossip about adult sex which Frankie angrily dismisses as "nasty lies" (pp. 1–11).

Yet even she has participated in a secret and unknown sin with a neighborhood boy in his garage, and she is sickened with guilt. Her father has decided she is too old to sleep with him, but she is afraid in her bed by herself. Her most vividly realized fear derives from the changes in her body which she epitomizes in her height. At her present rate of growth she calculates that she will end up over nine feet tall—a freak.

Frankie's fear of freaks surely indicates some subconscious understanding of the qualities within herself which make her peculiar in the eyes of the normal world. McCullers uses the motif of unfinished music to underline and intensify Frankie's dilemma, suggesting the proper resolution to her confused view of herself. In Part 1, Frankie hears a grieving blues tune on "the sad horn of some colored boy" at night. The disembodied sound expresses her own feelings, for she herself is a piece of unfinished music. Just as the tune approaches its conclusion, the horn suddenly stops playing. The music's incompleteness drives Frankie wild, trapping inside her the unbearable emotions it has drawn to a focus (pp. 41–42). Like Mick Kelly, Frankie tries to find release through masochism, beating her head with her fist, as she will do again several times in the story. When she changes her name to the romantic F. Jasmine in Part 2 and waltzes around town in a dress, telling everyone she meets that her brother and his bride will take her away with them on their wedding trip, the unfinished music is resolved in her mind. Her stories about the wedding sound inside her "as the last chord of a guitar murmurs a long time after the strings are struck." Unfortunately, her fantasies of the wedding are doomed to disappointment. We know this long before the event because McCullers returns to the motif of unfinished music, this time in the sound made by a piano tuner at work, which embodies F. Jasmine's romantic dream. "Then in a dreaming way a chain of chords climbed slowly upward *like a flight of castle stairs*: but just at the end, when the eighth chord should have sounded and the scale made complete, there was a stop" (p. 81, my emphasis).

The only event that resolves the unfinished music as well as the frantic, disjointed activities of F. Jasmine, John Henry, and Berenice is the transcendent moment when a group of older girls file slowly through the backyard in clean, fresh dresses and are turned golden by the slanting rays of the evening sun. These girls are a sublime vision of Frankie–F. Jasmine's destiny, a vision of ideal feminine grace before which the group in the kitchen stands transfixed in hushed awe. The piano tuner is silent. F. Jasmine's growing body and the outside world demand that she complete herself in the terms of this vision, but she will not submit until her fantasies of escape are smashed.

The meaning of the unfinished music is closely linked to Frankie's spiritual kinship with the blacks of her little Southern town. Both are made clear in the person of Honey Brown, Berenice's young, light-skinned foster brother. Too intelligent and restless to live comfortably in the circumscribed world of Sugarville, the black section of town, he periodically explodes: "Honey played the horn, and he had been first in his studies at the colored high school. He ordered a French book from Atlanta and learned himself some French. At the same time he would suddenly run hog-wild all over Sugarville and tear around for several days, until his friends would bring him home more dead than living" (p 122). The old black fortune-teller Big Mama explains that God withdrew His hand before Honey was completed, leaving him eternally unsatisfied. It must have been Honey's sad blues horn that Frankie heard in the night, the horn that stopped playing just short of the music's resolution. Big Mama's explanation of Honey's plight describes his frustration clearly enough, but the real cause of Honey's problems is the fact that he, like Frankie, does not fit the categories imposed on him by his Southern town.

Frankie shares a sense of entrapment with Honey and Berenice, but hers is not finally as severe, even though it is more vividly realized in the novel. At first she longs to escape from her hot, stultified town to the cold, snowy peace of Alaska. At the end of Part 1, however, she fixes on the wedding in Winter Hill as the means of escape. The old question of who she is and what she will become ceases to torment her when she decides to be a member of the wedding and go out into the world with her brother and his bride. This absurd fantasy is a denial of the adult sexuality which Frankie cannot bear to acknowledge, but her attraction to it is obvious in her infatuation with the engaged couple. McCullers associates the returning motif of unfinished music with the imagery of prison to show that F. Jasmine's romantic dream will not bring escape. The evening before the wedding, when the piano tuner repeats again and again his unfinished chords, "the bars of sunlight crossed the back yard like the bars of a bright strange jail" (p. 75). In the crazily disoriented recent months, Frankie had feared the eyes of the prisoners in the town jail because she sensed that they, like the freaks at the fair, recognized her as one of them. Even as F. Jasmine, she is closer to them than she knows. Berenice explains that all human beings are imprisoned in their separate bodies and separate minds, blacks even more extremely than others.

> We all of us somehow caught. We born this way or that way and we don't know why. But we caught anyhow. I born Berenice. You born Frankie. John Henry born John Henry. And maybe we wants to widen and bust free. But no matter what we do we still caught.... But they done drawn completely extra bounds around all colored people. They done squeezed us off in one corner by ourself.... Sometimes a boy like Honey feel like he just can't breathe no more. He feel like he got to break something or break himself. [pp. 113–14]

F. Jasmine feels like breaking things too, but her frustration usually expresses itself rather harmlessly in perverse moods. She is ultimately able to accept the limitations of her sex, which of course are far less cramped than the restrictions of segregation in the 1940s. But McCullers is making a traditional association between the oppression of women and that of blacks, an association most obvious in Harriet Beecher Stowe's *Uncle Tom's Cabin* in the nineteenth century, but also very clear in the relationship of the recent feminist movement to the Civil Rights Movement of the 1960s.[21]

Frankie is caught in a blossoming female body which she must recognize and accept. She must also face the fact that grown men and women make love, and that her body makes her desirable to men. As a younger child she had unwittingly walked in on the lovemaking of a man and his wife who were boarders in her house. Uncomprehending, she thought the man was having a fit. Even at twelve she does not understand the nature of his convulsions, just as she refuses to listen to the "nasty lies" of the older girls and tries not to think of her own wicked experience in the neighbor boy's garage. This innocence makes her dangerously vulnerable when as F. Jasmine she wanders through the town looking older and wiser than her years. The toughness that had served her well as a tomboy betrays her now, so that the soldier she meets in the Blue Moon Cafe assumes she is willing to be seduced. F. Jasmine is paralyzed with horror as the soldier embraces her in his cheap hotel room. She feels she is in the Crazy House at the fair or in the insane asylum at Milledgeville. At the last minute she knocks him out with a pitcher and makes her getaway down the fire escape. Not until late the next night, after the disaster of the wedding, does her mind accept the meaning of this encounter and its relation to her veiled sexual memories and anxieties. By then her brother and his bride have rejected her and she has suffered the humiliation of being pulled screaming from the steering wheel of their car. Back home, she has made a futile attempt to run away and has been recovered by her father in the Blue Moon Cafe, where she had felt she was drowning.

The Member of the Wedding ends in a new world, with Frances reborn as a giddy adolescent. The environment of her childhood has been dismantled completely—John Henry has died horribly of meningitis, Berenice has resigned herself to marriage and quit her job, and Frances is preparing to move to a new house with her father. The final scene takes place in the kitchen, now remodeled so that it is unrecognizable as the freakish prison of the terrible summer. Frances is making dainty sandwiches to serve her new soulmate, an artistic girl two years her senior. No longer a frightened alien, she is united with her friend through a mutual infatuation with poetry and art.

Notes

20. Moers, 109; *The Member of the Wedding*, 77–78. Subsequent references will be indicated parenthetically by page number in my text.

21. See Moers, 19–41.

KENNETH D. CHAMLEE ON THE FUNCTION OF THE CAFÉ SETTING IN THE DEVELOPMENT OF CHARACTER

Carson McCullers seldom uses the natural landscape as an important physical or symbolic setting in her fiction. Instead of the deltas, forests, and worn-out farms of her contemporaries Eudora Welty and Flannery O'Connor, McCullers prefers to place her stories in bedrooms, dining rooms, hospital and hotel rooms, bars, kitchens, and cafés. Although it would be inaccurate to say that Welty and O'Connor seldom interiorize settings, Louise Westling has noted that McCullers almost always does so.[1] This tendency towards enclosure is further evidenced by the inwardness of characters like Biff Brannon, Frankie Addams, and Amelia Evans. Though many of her protagonists spend time in self-absorbed isolation, McCullers always emphasizes their search to belong, to find some context of community and love. Joseph Millichap says that in

McCullers' fiction "the search for personal realization must necessarily be social because [man] must communicate with and love other human beings."[2]

One interior social setting that McCullers frequently employs in this search for self-realization is the café. In her most important novels, *The Heart Is A Lonely Hunter*, *The Member of the Wedding*, and *The Ballad of the Sad Café*, McCullers uses cafés as centers of activity whose varied social atmospheres reflect the personalities apparent in their owners. While both owners and patrons are part of McCullers' parade of deformed and confused people seeking human connections, cafés ultimately provide a false sense of emotional security and fail to give characters the lasting acceptance and feeling of community they desire.

The cafés in these three novels typify their owners' interests and personalities and help demonstrate McCullers' tendency to populate her work with grotesques who are seeking to belong somewhere.

(...)

The Blue Moon Café of *The Member of the Wedding* has a somewhat different function from that of Biff Brannon's diner. Not a central site in the novel's action, only four scenes occur there, each involving the protagonist Frankie Addams. The Blue Moon is a combination bar and hotel, whose Portuguese owner, a minor character, has settled for a life without personal involvements. His indifference not only encourages altercations which bring the police but accounts for the lack of supervision which allows minors like Frankie to be served beer and led upstairs to rented rooms.

At the beginning of the novel Frankie is a member of a real community—the kitchen family of Berenice and John Henry—but she does not cherish that familiar world any longer: "The name for what had happened to her Frankie did not know, but she could feel her squeezed heart beating against the table edge";[10] "this was the summer that Frankie was sick and tired of being Frankie" (pp. 19–20).[11] Her current growth spurt has caused her to project her eventual height to be over nine feet tall, which would make her as bizarre as something in the Chattahoochee Exposition Freak House. Struggling with the changes in her body and emotions, Frankie says "I wish I was somebody else except me" (p. 6). In her determination to break free, Frankie latches onto an impending change in the family structure, her brother Jarvis' marriage to Janice Evans, and imagines herself becoming an integral part of the union and escaping with the newlyweds to Alaska, Africa, Burma, and other exotic places. Her subsequent announcement of those intentions meets with disbelieving taunts from Berenice, so Frankie decides to share her plans with strangers while on a walking tour around the town, what she thinks will be her last look at the dreary city. Her decision not to return after the wedding also prompts a change in her self-identity; she is no longer the childish Frankie but the mature F. Jasmine.

The Blue Moon Café is an adult world from which Frankie has previously felt excluded ("a place for holiday soldiers and the grown and free" [p. 53]) but in which she now feels welcome; thus, it is the first place F. Jasmine chooses to reveal her plans. As Ihab Hassan notes, "the animating center of the novel, the unifying force in Frankie's character, is ... her wish to belong."[12] Beneath the "blue neon lights" that make faces turn "pale green" (p. 53), F. Jasmine tells her story to the Blue Moon's owner and believes she is communicating with him because "it is far easier ... to convince strangers of the coming to pass of dearest wants than those in your own home kitchen" (p. 54). But she might as well be talking to the dead: "The Portuguese listened with his head cocked to one side, his dark eyes ringed with ash-gray circles, and now and then he wiped his damp veined dead-white hands on his stained apron" (p. 54). When F. Jasmine is finished, the Portuguese does not speak, so she wanders out to tell others about her plans. She meets the red-headed soldier and returns with him to the Blue Moon, but she does not communicate any better with him than with the owner. Obviously misjudging her age, the dissolute soldier ignores F. Jasmine's prattle while occasionally dropping stale come-on lines—"I could of sworn I'd run into you some place before" (p. 67)—which F. Jasmine is too naive to recognize or understand. The most serious miscommunication, though, occurs when F. Jasmine returns to the Blue Moon that night for her "date" and, confused by the soldier's double talk, goes upstairs with him. Never fully understanding his intentions, she fights his sexual advances instinctively, knocks him out with a water pitcher, and flees.

The next night, after the disastrous wedding scene, Frances (as she now calls herself) is so embarrassed and hurt that she decides to run away and once again ends up at the Blue Moon. But the day's humiliation has left her drained and spiritless. Confronted by a policeman who is looking for her, she no longer sees the café as any avenue of escape or change: "What am I doing in here?" she repeated. For all at once she had forgotten, and she told the truth when she said finally, "I don't know" (p. 147). Before she goes home with her father, the Portuguese, owner glances at her, "and there was in those eyes no feeling of connection" (p. 148). Though Frankie Addams initially feels the Blue Moon Café is a place where she can assert her new adult identity and make the human contacts she desires, it turns out to be a sterile place characterized by its ghostly, apathetic proprietor, a place where Frankie is more isolated in her adolescence than ever before.

Notes

1. Louise Westling, *Sacred Groves and Ravaged Gardens: The Fiction of Eudora Welty, Carson McCullers, and Flannery O'Connor* (Athens: Univ. of Georgia Press, 1985), p. 6.

2. Joseph R. Millichap, "The Realistic Structure of *The Heart Is a Lonely Hunter*," *TCL*, 17 (1971), 17.

10. Carson McCullers, *The Member of the Wedding* (New York: Bantam, 1986), p. 4. Subsequent references, noted parenthetically, are to this edition.

11. If cafés typify the failure of community in McCullers' novels, kitchens are often the centers of social warmth, frequently presided over by Faulknerian black matriarchs. Both Portia in *The Heart Is A Lonely Hunter* and Berenice in *The Member of the Wedding* fulfill nurturing, mother-like roles to Mick Kelly and Frankie Addams, respectively. Even

Amelia Evens in *The Ballad of the Sad Café* shows such tendencies, charitably feeding Cousin Lymon in her kitchen on the night vt his arrival.

12. Hassan, p. 321.

VIRGINIA SPENCER CARR ON THE BIOGRAPHICAL AND LITERARY CONTEXTS

Frankie Addams was not McCullers's mirror image as an adolescent, but she was close kin in every important aspect of character and being. She and Mick, the youthful protagonist in *The Heart Is a Lonely Hunter*, evolved with much in common, having come from the same environment and social class as McCullers herself. Both are daughters of tired, wan jewelers who had hoped for far more satisfaction in their lives and careers than they actually have. The only maternal nurturing each girl receives is from the black servant (and surrogate mother) in her household. Mick has Portia Copeland and Frankie has the one-eyed Berenice Sadie Brown. Mick's mother is too busy operating her boardinghouse to be concerned with the emotional rearing of her daughter, and Frankie's mother has died in childbirth. In their restless approach to puberty, both girls fend largely for themselves. The unnamed fictional towns in which Mick and Frankie live are not unlike McCullers's own hometown as she knew it in the late 1930s. Frankie's peregrinations carry her up and down the four blocks of Front Avenue, the actual name for the street that runs parallel to McCullers's own main street, Broadway, in Columbus, Georgia. Frankie's town, too, has an army post like Fort Benning tucked into its lower pocket.

McCullers employed the same straightforward, omniscient narrative voice in *The Member of the Wedding* that had served her well in *The Heart Is a Lonely Hunter* and *Reflections in a Golden Eye*. But the voice here is more singular, personal, and poignant. *The Member of the Wedding* is Frankie's story—she is the member—and every significant event in the novel relates to her. This novel is also the most compressed in time of all of

McCullers's long works, including her next, and final, novel, *Clock Without Hands* (1961).

The three-part structure of *The Member of the Wedding* is much like the structure of *The Heart Is a Lonely Hunter*, and in each novel there is one main event: the suicide of John Singer and the wedding of Frankie's brother. Like McCullers's first novel, *The Member of the Wedding* was planned according to a precise and harmonious design enriched by the contrapuntal fugue-like voices of the main characters.[2] In part 1, Frankie suddenly realizes who she is and where she is going. She is in love with the bride and her brother and plans to accompany them on their honeymoon, wherever it may be. Part 2 takes place the day before the wedding as the exuberant Frankie makes her plans to leave; she bids farewell to her town as though it has been poised to hear from her in her new identity as "F. Jasmine Addams." Frankie had made up the name *Jasmine* to strengthen the bond (alliteratively) with her brother and his bride, Jarvis and Janice. Part 3, strikingly like its counterpart in *The Heart Is a Lonely Hunter* both in length and importance to the action that precedes it, is a brief coda that reports the events after the wedding when Frankie painfully discovers the reality of the situation and is dragged from the honeymoon car.

In *The Heart Is a Lonely Hunter*, each character realizes upon the death of John Singer that if he is to survive he must be his own person and not the reflection of what he thinks he had seen in the deaf mute. More resilient than Mick, Frankie shores up her fragments and finds solace in a new friendship with someone her age. Frankie still has her illusions, but she accepts herself, no longer wishes to be a member of the opposite sex, and begins to go by her real name, *Frances*.

When the story opens, Frankie looks like a boy. Her hair is short, she is barefoot, and she is dressed in a pair of blue track shorts and a B.V.D. undershirt. On the edge of puberty, she yearns for a connection that will get her out of the kitchen and away from the house, where her only companions are her six-year-old cousin, John Henry West, and Berenice Sadie Brown, the housekeeper and cook who entertains Frankie and her cousin as best she can. Frankie vaguely admires her father, but finds him too preoccupied with his watch repair and jeweler's business to supervise or nurture her in any meaningful way. When she tells him (in part 2) that she will not come home after the wedding, he does not listen, but querulously demands to know what has happened to his monkey wrench and screw driver.

Throughout the novel, Frankie is caught between the injunctions of those in authority in her life, who demand that she exercise common sense and reason, and her own desperate need to fantasize about a connection with something larger than herself. Despite Royal Addams's gruff nature and apparent insensitivity to his daughter's needs, McCullers treats him sympathetically. Addams is, in fact, as close a rendering of her own father as the author dared put on paper. Frankie notes that her father "walked the dawn-stale kitchen like a person who has lost something, but has forgotten what it is that he has lost. Watching him, the old grudge was forgotten, and she felt sorry."[3]

Berenice cannot relieve the child's ambivalent and unfulfilled yearnings, although she is a nurturing and healthy influence on Frankie. Berenice instructs Frankie in motherly fashion, but her stoic acceptance of her own "caught condition" in a white man's world makes it impossible for her to understand thoroughly the child's troubled nature and her schemes to effect some kind of meaningful change in her life. As if speaking for all of her fictional brethren who inhabit the landscape of McCullers's novels and short stories, Berenice says, "We all of us somehow caught. We born this way or that way and we don't know why" (98). She makes it clear to Frankie that her skin color adds another dimension to the problems that must be faced in life: "But they done drawn completely extra bounds around all colored people. They done squeezed us off in one corner by ourself" (98).

John Henry—a spectator to most of the events—is reminiscent of Mick Kelly in his penchant for queer, childish drawings with which he has covered Frankie's kitchen walls as high as he can reach. The shabby kitchen with its strange decorations has the look of a "crazy house," and Frankie is vaguely afraid. "The world is certainly a sudden place" (6), she announces to Berenice and John Henry, having just learned that Jarvis is getting married to a girl from Winter Hill, Georgia. His coming from Alaska, where he was stationed in the army, and marrying a girl from a small town in his home state is a curious coincidence, thinks Frankie, whose mind leaps to thoughts of Eskimos, snow, frozen seas, and polar bears. The fact that John Henry has seen snow gives him a special status that she herself woefully lacks, a status that makes his presence more acceptable to her. Frankie often joins John Henry and Berenice at the kitchen table for three-handed bridge, and in their boredom they sometimes lay down their cards and begin to "criticize the Creator" and tell each other how, if they were God, they would improve the world.

Just as the soul rots with boredom in Amelia's mill town in *The Ballad of the Sad Café*, so, too, does Frankie's during the "dog days" of summer in her microcosmic world of the kitchen. Because her country is at war (the action of the novel is compressed into four months during the first year or two of World War II), Frankie wants to be a Marine and win gold medals for bravery (her inability to actually "join the war" intensifies her restlessness and makes her even more irrational). She fantasizes giving a quart of blood a week—still another means of attaining kinship—so that it "would be in the veins of Australians and Fighting French and Chinese, all over the whole world" (20).

While McCullers was writing this part of *The Member of the Wedding*, New York City was experiencing a wartime blackout, and she imagined women being conscripted to military service and herself going overseas as a soldier or a foreign correspondent. In the spring of 1943, she wrote friends that she had "gone to the top" in trying to get hired as an overseas reporter, but those who knew of her efforts did not take them seriously.[4] She spoke, too, of adopting a war orphan, but that effort—or "whim," as some called it—did not materialize, either. Similarly, Frankie is "rejected" by the war, the blood bank, and her father as well, who asks: "Who is this great big long-legged twelve-year-old blunderbuss who still wants to sleep with her old Papa?" (20). In retaliation for this rejection and other imagined slights, Frankie tells Berenice that she would like to "tear down" the whole town.

In an essay entitled "Love's Not Time's Fool," published in *Mademoiselle* in 1943, McCullers took the stance of a war wife, having recently received what she described as a "noble conciliatory letter" from Reeves McCullers in which he declared that he still loved her and was over his "strange sickness" that had made him do the "ignoble things" that led to their estrangement.[5] After their divorce, he had gone back into the army, was now a second lieutenant, and would soon be going overseas, Reeves wrote her. McCullers, too, was of a different heart. Annemarie Clarac-Schwarzenbach had died in a bicycle accident in Switzerland over a year earlier, and McCullers was receptive to a "new Reeves," she declared.[6]

In her personal life as in her fiction, McCullers tried relentlessly to drive away her demons and to commit herself to something beyond her own separate being. Just as Mick wanted to be a member of a "bunch," so, too, does Frankie, but she fears that the only group into which she can fit is the troupe of freaks at the midway of the county fair. She had stood with John Henry in front of the booth of the "Half-Man Half-Woman" and imagined that all of the freaks were watching her in a "secret way" and trying to connect their eyes with hers as though to say "we know you" (17). Frankie is drawn, too, to the jail, where she feels the eyes of the convicts upon her as she walks back and forth in front of the barred windows. "Do you think I will grow into a Freak?" she asks Berenice. "Certainly not, I trust Jesus," replies Berenice (18). But Frankie does not have Berenice's faith. Again and again, Frankie asks herself where she could possibly go to become the kind of person she envisions herself.

In focusing on the issues that lie at the heart of Frankie's identity crisis, the narrator discusses her aloneness in light of the companionship that everyone else seems to have in his or her life:

She was an I person who had to walk around and do things by herself. All other people had a *we* to claim, all others except her. When Berenice said *we*, she meant Honey and Big Mama, her lodge, or her church. The *we* of her father was the store. All members of dubs have a *we* to belong to and to talk about. The soldiers in the army can say *we*, and even the criminals on chaingangs. But the old Frankie had had no *we* to claim, unless it would be the terrible summer *we* of her and John Henry and Berenice—and that was the last *we* in the world she wanted (35).

Suddenly, Frankie has an epiphany, an illumination not unlike McCullers's own as she chased after the fire engine with Gypsy Rose Lee. Frankie decides that her brother and his bride are her "*we of me*," a realization that causes her "squeezed heart" to suddenly open and divide. She tells John Henry that she is going off with them after the wedding and "to whatever place that they will ever go.... It's like I've known it all my life, that I belong to be with them. I love the two of them so much" (38).

On the day before the wedding as Frankie, Berenice, and John Henry sit and talk in the kitchen, Frankie is distracted by the tuning of the piano in the next room. The tuner plays repeatedly the scale "up until the seventh note," then hesitates there, unable to finish. Frankie thinks it strange that the "G" and "A" notes are so markedly different since they are "side by side there on the piano just as close together as the other notes" (89), and her thoughts of separateness return. "Doesn't it strike you as strange that I am I, and you are you?" she demands of Berenice. "I am F. Jasmine Addams. And you are Berenice Sadie Brown. And we can look at each other, and touch each other, and stay together year in and year out in the same room. Yet always I am I, and you are you. And I can't ever be anything else but me, and you can't ever be anything else but you" (94).

Frankie tells Berenice that she wants to know everybody in the whole world, and that going off with Janice and Jarvis after the wedding will make it happen. Her obsession to be joined in a "we of me" with her brother and his bride is extended now to include the whole human race, and she is determined to become the sum of all she imagines. Her dream is destined to fail, of course, as surely as the soft August moths are caught in their "irony of fate," as Frankie refers to their plight, when, attracted by the light, they press against the window screen and die (12). At the wedding she discovers what she has secretly feared: that certain things will always be beyond her power. When her father ejects her, screaming, from the honeymoon car, Frankie is forced to admit defeat. Afterwards, she sits with Berenice in the back of the bus as they return home from Winter Hill. Overcome by self-hatred after taking momentary solace in thinking of the "mean word" she had never used before ("*nigger*"), she wants the "whole world to die" (118).

Frankie has been haunted during the course of her summer by several actual deaths of people in her town. One was the murder of a young black boy who was found dead behind her father's store, his slashed throat open "like a crazy shivering mouth that spoke ghost words into the April sun" (76). McCullers's image foreshadows Frankie's own situation later, when she stands tongue-tied in the bride's room just before the wedding, yearning to say "I love the two of you so much and you are the we of me. Please take me with you from the wedding, for we belong to be together" (119), but she can utter not a word. The death of an uncle that summer had made her even more aware of her mortality, and in thinking of him, she remembers those she has known who have died who "feel nothing, hear nothing, see nothing: only black," and she is struck by the "terrible finality of it all" (77). Although she had declared earlier that she would shoot herself in the head with her father's pistol if the bride and her brother did not take her with them, she cannot pull the trigger because "deadness was blackness, nothing but pure terrible blackness that went on and on and never ended until the end of all the world" (125). Frankie is further shocked by the death of John Henry, who screams in pain for three days before dying of spinal meningitis.

Frankie's preoccupation with death was doubtless influenced by the deaths of three people in McCullers's own life while she was working on the novel. One of the children in her neighborhood, a little boy, died of spinal meningitis, and another, five-year-old Robin Mullin, who lived next door, drowned. Robin came often to the Smith family's kitchen for treats and lingered, much as John Henry did, feeling free to come and go because the same servant kept house and cooked for both households. Like John Henry, the child considered himself a "member of the kitchen."[7] The death that affected McCullers the most profoundly, however, was that of her father, whose body was found in his jewelry store on August 1, 1944. Although the newspapers reported it a heart attack, intimates of the family claimed that the melancholy jeweler had, in fact, shot himself.[8]

The night that Frankie returns from the wedding, bitter and angry, she writes her father a farewell letter in which she explains that she can stand her existence no longer. She takes the pistol from her father's bureau drawer and heads for the train station with a vague idea of jumping on any freight car that happened to come along, but the station is closed and there are no trains expected until morning. After walking the "night-empty streets" until she ends up in the alley where the youth was found that spring with his throat slashed, she decides to wait for the train at the bar of the Blue Moon, the hotel in which she had kept a "date" with a soldier and naively ended up in his room (she had cracked him over the head with a water pitcher to ward off his advances and told no one of her misadventure). When a policeman discovers her at the Blue Moon—her father having "sicked the Law on her"—and asks where she "was headed," Frankie pictures an enormous canyon between herself and all the places she has formerly envisioned. She recognizes that her "plans for the movies or the Marines were only child plans that would never work" and tries to think of the "littlest, ugliest place she knew, for to run away there could not be considered so very wrong. 'Flowering Branch,'" she replies (128).

In the novel's final scene, it is November and John Henry is dead. Frankie goes by "Frances" now and remembers her little cousin only as he used to be. The old familiar kitchen has been renovated, the house has been sold, and Frankie and her father are moving to a home in the suburbs that they will share with John Henry's parents. Berenice, too, is in the process of making changes. She has given "quit notice" to the Addams family and plans to marry again.

Frankie has not spoken once of her brother's wedding since that fateful day and devotes her time now to poetry, radar, school, and her new friend, Mary Littlejohn, who was once the "pasty-faced girl with pigtails" chosen instead of Frankie for club membership by the older girls in the neighborhood. She tells Berenice as they prepare to leave the kitchen for good that she and Mary are planning "to travel around the world together."

As she gazes out the window, awaiting the arrival of her friend, Frankie notices that the "last pale colors" of the day appear "crushed and cold on the horizon. Dark, when it came, would come on quickly, as it does in wintertime," interjects the narrator (132).

"I am simply mad about—" but Frances leaves the sentence unfinished, for "with an instant shock of happiness," she hears the "ringing of the bell" (132).

Desperate to escape the "caught condition" of which Berenice has spoken, Frankie.allows the "shock of happiness" to divert her attention from that which she is "mad about." However, given the deterministic theme that runs evenly through this and other works by McCullers, there is no reason to believe that Frankie's new-found contentment will be anything but short-lived.

Early reviews of *The Member of the Wedding* were, for the most part, laudatory. George Dangerfield recommended the book to readers of *The Saturday Review of Literature* as a "marvelous piece of writing" and called the author "unique." Although "nothing occurs here," he wrote, every page is "filled with a sense of something having happened, happening, and about to happen. This is in itself a considerable technical feat;

and, beyond that, there is magic in it."[9] Isa Kapp compared McCullers to Thomas Wolfe and informed readers of the *New York Times Book Review* that McCullers's language had the "freshness, quaintness and gentleness of a sensitive child."[10] Rarely had "emotional turbulence been so delicately conveyed," he added. Marguerite Young, writing for *The Kenyon Review*, called McCullers a "poetic symbolist, a seeker after those luminous meanings which always do transcend the boundaries of the stereotyped, the conventional, and the so-called normal."[11]

Notes

2. Carson McCullers, "The Vision Shared," *Theatre Arts* 34 (Apr. 1950): 30; reprinted in *The Mortgaged Heart*, 265.

3. McCullers, *The Member of the Wedding* (Boston: Houghton Mifflin, 1946), 44. All page references within the text are to this edition.

4. Carr, *The Lonely Hunter*, 227–228.

5. "Love's Not Time's Fool" (signed by "A War Wife"), *Mademoiselle*, 16 (Apr. 1943): 95.

6. Carr, 232.

7. Lamar Smith to Carr, interview, Perry, Fla., 3 Oct. 1970.

8. David Diamond and Vannie Copland Jackson to Carr, conversation, Columbus, Ga., 23 Oct. 1987. At the close of a symposium held at Columbus College in Columbus, Ga., to commemorate the twentieth anniversary of McCullers's death, intimates of McCullers (who had known her in her hometown or in New York) spoke freely about the alleged heart attack and said that Lamar Smith's death was "definitely a suicide."

9. George Dangerfield, "An Adolescent's Four Days," *The Saturday Review of Literature* (30 Mar. 1946): 15.

10. Isa Kapp, "One Summer: Three Lives," *New York Times Book Review* (24 Mar. 1946): 5.

11. Marguerite Young, "Metaphysical Fiction," *The Kenyon Review*, 9 (Winter 1947): 151–155.

Thadious M. Davis on
The Characterization(s) of Berenice in Two
Versions of the Novel

Race as a familiar sign of social difference figures prominently in modern southern literature, where the cultural network often represents "blackness" as an obverse reflection of the dominant culture's "whiteness." In *The Member of the Wedding*, Carson McCullers's 1946 novel, racialization encodes gender and expands the symbolic possibilities for representing both gender difference and identity formation. McCullers's play, *The Member of the Wedding* (1949, 1951), however, dramatically reveals a narrowing down of an author's vision to suit preconceived racial attitudes and prevalent gender notions of the time, as well as to suit the largest possible audience identification of comfortably familiar characters and stereotypical actions. While McCullers's novel may be read as an intervention in the prevailing mythologies naturalizing whiteness and heterosexuality, her play retreats to an accommodationist position that allows for a smaller register of difference not only for the white girl protagonist, but also for the black adults who participate in her rite of passage into adolescence. The novel, thus, is a project in defamiliarization, whereas the play can be understood as largely an exercise in familiarization.

(...)

Three years after the publication of *The Member of the Wedding*, McCullers completed a play based on her novel. In it she revisioned not Frankie and her cousin John Henry, but the blacks: Berenice, the cook-housekeeper; T.T. Williams, her suitor; and Honey Camden Brown, her foster-brother.[4] Berenice, whose reminiscences of her four marriages in the novel serve both to inform Frankie about the mistaken choices that adults make in trying to replicate a lost happiness and to warn Frankie about the dangers of compulsory heterosexuality, is initially a wise confidante. Although not entirely understanding the depths of Frankie's loneliness or her fears of being "queer" and therefore not "belonging," Berenice nonetheless knows that Frankie's life is in transition, that she is moving from girlhood to womanhood, that physically she is maturing rapidly, and that emotionally she is floundering.

This Berenice in the novel is a woman with a fixed "we of me," which Frankie envies. Berenice has a life of her own outside the Addams household; she has family and a suitor, her organizations and church. She has a social life in which she, T. T., and Honey go out to supper at the New Metropolitan Tea Room. She is secure in her sexual identity, as her revelations about marriage and the treatment of women and wives illustrate.

Berenice is also firmly rooted in her racial identity. Although she does not exaggerate racial differences, she is thoroughly aware of race as a factor of individual identification, as for example when she describes Frankie's brother Jarvis and his fiancee as "a good-looking blond white boy. And the girl is kind of brunette and small and pretty. They make a nice white couple" (27). Blind in one eye, Berenice does not misread the configurations of race in her society; she tells Frankie and John Henry that she is "caught worse" than they "[b]ecause I am black.... Because I am colored.... [T]hey done drawn completely extra bounds around all colored people. They done squeezed us off in one corner by ourself" (113–14). Berenice Sadie Brown is a rounded person with a connected, if not harmonious, past and, implicitly, with a future of her own, for at the end of the novel she is preparing to marry T.T. and has given notice that she will no longer work for the relocating Addams family. The novel ends by complicating received notions of racial difference.[5]

In the play, however, the ideological assumptions maintain racial hierarchies and conventions. There is no intervention in the existing system of representation of blacks, and no disruption of conventional portraits of blacks. There is, instead, a distorting of the lives created in the novel in order to access and claim the expected and the familiar. Berenice's role in assisting Frankie's transformation to adulthood is undermined. In fact, she becomes almost childlike herself. She is coarse, insisting for instance that she has a right to as much fun as anyone, that she has not gone through the change of life. "Fun" is equated with sexual intercourse, and menopause is used to demarcate age and the cessation of sexual pleasure. McCullers emphasized both Berenice's sexuality and her subservience, so that we hear Berenice say that she won't marry T.T. because "he don't make me shiver none" (72), and we watch her upbraid Honey for being impudent to whites and for not addressing her employer Mr. Addams as "sir" (68). Sexualized, racialized, and objectified, Berenice Sadie Brown in the dramatic text cannot become a subject.[6]

Notes

4. The members of the Addams family have expanded roles in the play: Mr. Addams, Jarvis and his fiancée, Aunt Pet (Mrs. West, John Henry's mother) all appear. See Carson McCullers, *The Member of the Wedding: A Play* (New York: New Directions, 1951); hereafter cited in the text.

5. Richard M. Cook, for example, observes that when Richard Wright "praised McCullers for being able 'to handle Negro characters with as much ease and justice as chose of her own race,' he was praising her for revealing beneath the stereotypes valuable complex human beings— people interesting in the variousness of their contradictions as well as in their suffering" (*Carton McCullers* [New York: Frederick Ungar, 1975], 128).

6. At the same time, however, the stage presence of the actress Ethel Waters, appearing as Berenice in the first New York production (opening January 5, 1950, at the Empire Theater), ameliorated somewhat the stereotyped Berenice of the play. Her performance, although adhering co the type McCullers created for the stage, gave the character a greater stature and more human dimension than the text implied.

TONY JASON STAFFORD ON THE MOTIF OF SIGHT IN THE PLAY VERSION

In *The Lonely Hunter*, Virginia Carr's biography of Carson McCullers, the author notes that McCullers, in her desire for warmth and tenderness from those around her, habitually used her eyes as a way of "communicating a closeness that denied actual physical touching, yet mirrored in one's pupils the exchange of souls" (296). Carr also observes that McCullers "always looked intently at a person she loved" and especially at the eyes, which she "gazed fixedly into" (296). Interestingly enough, this same personal habit of gazing fixedly at someone appears in the autobiographical character of Frankie Adams in McCullers' *The Member of the Wedding*, and McCullers uses Frankie's pattern of behavior, along with other vision motifs, as a way of leading the reader/viewer into a better understanding of the play's more elusive concerns.

The opening stage directions of the play describe Frankie Addams as "standing in the arbor gazing adoringly at her brother Jarvis and his fiancee Janice" (1). Casual and trivial though the action may seem, the stage picture of Frankie staring intently at someone becomes, through numerous repetitions, an action fraught with meaning. It is, among other things, a ploy on Frankie's behalf to be noticed and thus included not only in this couple's relationship but in the relationships of others as well. Moreover, this opening tableau establishes through the action of the eyes a visual motif that functions as an integral part of the play's language and provides a context for a deeper insight into the play's philosophical import.

A close study of the opening scene reveals that Frankie's chief action throughout the scene is gazing silently at the couple. Frankie, after the opening tableau, apparently is to hold her position until the time for her to help Berenice serve drinks; when she has finished serving, she then, according to McCullers' stage directions, "perches on the ground before Janice and Jarvis and stares adoringly at them" (3), which she continues to do during the ensuing conversation. Yet again, just before the scene closes, Frankie lets "her look linger on Janice and Jarvis" and, linking the deed with the feeling, languidly announces that "I never believed in love until now" (8–9). Soon afterwards, Jarvis stands up and "gazes fondly around the yard and arbor" and then "pulls [Janice] up and stands with his arm around her, gazing around him" (10). As the scene ends, a telling stage picture is presented: Frankie gazes fondly upon the couple but is not included, while Janice and Jarvis together gaze at the arbor and exclude Frankie from their embrace. It is a foreshadowing of the painful experience that lies ahead.

While visual imagery occurs in a limited way in McCullers' novel, she has in translating her narrative to the dramatic form responded to the stage's need for physical action by expanding the act of staring into a recurring deed, accompanying that behavior with a number of allusions to eyes, sight, and related matters. Moreover, eyes and sight are the subject of more than a few conversations, including discussions of physical sight and eyes, the use of "seeing" words as a metaphor for various mental activities, talk of superstitions and folklore about seeing and eyes, and stories of things seen and unseen.

Ultimately, the visual motif leads into a deeper sense of the play's themes, which are, as McCullers herself has said, about "moral isolation" (Carr, *Hunter*, 335) and "the will to belong" (Carr, *Hunter*, 341). Everything from the title itself to the last scene concerns Frankie's desire to belong to somebody or some group, especially to Janice and Jarvis, as a way of overcoming her feelings of isolation and loneliness. Frankie, it appears, is close to the philosophical position of Bishop Berkeley, who holds that "existence is identical with perception: *esse = percipi*"; he adds, "to say that things exist when no mind perceives them is perfectly unintelligible. Hence, to exist means to be perceived" (Thilly 360–61). Frankie seems to modify Berkeley's view to fit her own situation: to be included one must first be seen, and if one is not seen, one cannot possibly be included. While she may be sure that as long as a person is not seen one is definitely not included, she also presumes the opposite—that therefore to be seen is to be included. Her supposition is of course false, and the drive of the play is toward exposing its invalidity. On yet another level, the play is about the isolation and solitude of the human condition in general, and the song, "His Eye Is On The Sparrow," draws upon sight imagery in order to articulate this larger concern.

(...)

In one scene involving her cousin John Henry, whose "gold rimmed spectacles ... give him an oddly judicious look" (2), Frankie spends valuable stage time giving him a seeing test and concludes that "if I were you I'd just throw those glasses away. You can see good as anybody" (24). While it may at first seem difficult to justify the scene in terms of length of action, on the other hand, it does contribute to the development of the vision motif and builds on other action related to seeing and looking. When Berenice reprimands her, Frankie explains that she was only doing it for John Henry's "own good" because the glasses "don't look becoming" (24), a fact which, in Frankie's mind, could endanger his acceptability. The subject of John Henry's vision closes with Frankie saying, "I bet Janice and Jarvis are members of a lot of clubs" (24). While it may sound like a non sequitur, in Frankie's mind it is logical that the subject of eyes and seeing brings thoughts of belonging.

Other kinds of sight references are linked with John Henry. Immediately following the scene above, John Henry initiates a discussion of Berenice's "new glass eye" by searching in her purse for it. When he wearies of that conversation, he turns to "pickin at the doll's eyes," which Frankie tells him to take "somewhere out of my sight" (27), acting upon her belief that not to see is to reject. She rejects the doll, even though it is a gift from Jarvis, because she believes it is a child's toy. Finally, it is John Henry who asks the pregnant question, "is the glass eye your mind's eye?" (91) and creates the telling refrain, "grey eyes is glass" (79).

Frankie's conversations with Berenice are replete with allusions to sight, including discussions of Berenice's glass eye, each's claim to be able to "see" into the mind of the other, Berenice's stories of how vision experiences initiated each of her troubled affairs with men, and Frankie's matching tales of her own sight experiences.

Although Berenice sometimes wears a glass eye, at the beginning of the play she is wearing a black patch over the empty eye socket, a circumstance which, in addition to drawing attention to the eyes at the beginning of the play, immediately communicates the fact that her physical sight is impaired by at least fifty per cent and that to Berenice, as to anyone visually impaired, eyes and sight are matters of importance. But Berenice, it soon becomes apparent, compensates with other kinds of vision. Moreover, the glass eye itself figures prominently in several discussions, as, for example, when John Henry initiates a discussion by digging it out of Berenice's purse. While Berenice is inserting the eye, John Henry remarks that "the blue glass eye looks very cute," but Frankie opines that "I don't see why you had to get that eye. It has a wrong expression—let alone being blue" (25). When John Henry asks which of Berenice's eyes has better vision, Berenice explains that her glass eye, her right eye, "don't do me no seeing good at all" (25). Still, "I like the glass eye better," John Henry insists, "it is so bright and shiny—a real pretty eye" (25). Suddenly, with all this talk of eyes, Frankie inevitably makes the association: "Janice and Jarvis. It gives me this pain just to think about them" (25). Berenice then closes the subject by again alluding to eyes: "It is a known truth that gray-eyed people, are jealous" (25).

The image of the glass eye begins to be applied in other ways and thus to acquire broader significance. Berenice claims, for example, that "I can see right through them two gray eyes of yours like they was glass" (79), to which John Henry responds by chanting the refrain, "gray eyes is glass" (79). Frankie in turn "tenses her brows and looks steadily at Berenice" while Berenice continues, "I see what you have in mind ... I see through them eyes" (80). John Henry repeats his refrain twice more, "gray eyes is glass," "gray eyes is glass" (81). And a syllogism is created: gray eyes are glass, Frankie's eyes are gray, ergo, Frankie's eyes are glass, metaphorically speaking; glass eyes, as Berenice has already established, "don't do ... no seeing good at all." More specifically, glass eyes, i.e., Frankie's gray eyes, are ineffective in their looking, and this fact precludes Frankie's staring her way into Janice's and Jarvis' union, even though Frankie's "glass eyes" do allow Berenice to see through them, figuratively speaking, and know what Frankie is thinking.

(...)

Throughout the rest of the play, sight allusions appear randomly in support of the eye motif. The stage directions on some dozen occasions use words such as "stare," "gaze," "watch," "look," "glance," and "glimpse" to describe Frankie's behavior, and the object of her sight is either Berenice, people passing through her yard, the room, or, most often, the mirror, in which she either practices her staring or regards her "looks." She dreams of her life with the couple and the time when they will be called upon to give "an eye witness account about something" (61). Finally, she muses over the phenomenon of passing a stranger in the street when "the eyes make a connection" and then "you never see each other again ... not in your whole life" (86). Without realizing it, she has admitted once again the inefficacy of eyes in establishing connections.

After the wedding and after her father has "hauled her off the wedding car," which she had forced her way into, Frankie is escorted by her father into the kitchen where she "flings herself on the kitchen chair and sobs with her head in her arms on the kitchen table" (99). When Janice and Jarvis return to console her, she refuses to look at them and "keeps her face buried in her arms and does not look up," in which position she stubbornly remains while they plead with her. This tableau is the reverse of the opening one in which Frankie stared "adoringly" into the faces of these same people, but the logic is the same, although conversely applied: I cannot be looked at because "I am not included." Janice begs Frankie not to "hide your sweet face from us" and to "sit up." When Frankie eventually "raises her head slowly," she "stares with a look of wonder and misery," and as Janice and Jarvis exit, she "still stares at them as they go down the hall" (100). The only use for eyes now is to watch them leave, thus confirming that she is excluded and that staring has failed to gain her admission into the relationship.

Frankie, on the verge of puberty, can be seen in the course of the play as developing an expanding awareness not only of mating and sexual union but of a larger world beyond the familiar kitchen and the intimacy of Berenice and John Henry. She is given to adolescent philosophizing and seeks to make abstractions based on her limited experiences with life: she wonders about identity— "doesn't it strike you as strange that you are you and I am I?" (85); about time "while we're talking right now, this minute is passing. And ... no power on earth can bring it back again" (91); and about the ultimate isolation of human beings—"there are all these people I will never know" (86). Moreover, the world of which Frankie is becoming aware is a "sudden place." She is beginning to see that it is a society in which there is bigotry, violence, and injustice (e.g., Honey Camden's encounters with the legal system), that it is a world in which the atomic bomb has been exploded, and that life is haunted by the spectre of death (Berenice enlightens Frankie and John Henry with a simple fact of life, "everybody has to die" [71]).

(...)

This invocation of divine gazing deepens the sight motif. The loneliness, isolation, and terror that fill the three characters as they huddle around the kitchen table may be seen as an analogue for the human condition in general. To this extent, *The Member of the Wedding* echoes the personal angst of Carson McCullers; apparently, McCullers often felt a sense of alienation from an indifferent God. Carr points out that McCullers suffered from "a sense of abandonment, a loss of God and godliness which haunted her, intermittently, much of her life" (*Hunter* 194). Carr cites several incidents that give testimony to McCullers' theological views, but one of the most dramatic occurred one evening when McCullers was sitting around with a group of other writers at the Yaddo Colony and, apropos of nothing, suddenly cried out, "I've lost the presence of God!" (195). Such deep feelings of despair seem to be behind the metaphysical statement of the play and to underscore the irony of the comfort found in the song by the three characters, all of which is brought out through an examination of eye and sight imagery.

Works Cited

Carr, Virginia Spencer. *The Lonely Hunter: A Biography of Carson McCullers*. New York: Carroll and Graf Publishers, Inc., 1985.

———. *Understanding Carson McCullers*. Columbia: University of South Carolina Press, 1990.

Evans, Oliver. *The Ballad of Carson McCullers: A Biography*. New York: Coward-McCann, Inc., 1966.

McBride, Mary. "Loneliness and Longing in Selected Plays of Carson McCullers and Tennessee Williams." *Modern American Drama: The Female Canon*. Rutherford, NJ: Fairleigh Dickinson University Press, 1990.

McCullers, Carson. *The Member of the Wedding: A Play*. New York: New Directions Books, 1951.

Thilly, Frank. *A History of Philosophy*. New York: Henry Holt and Company, 1952.

Weales, Gerald. *American Drama Since World War II*. New York: Harcourt, Brace, and World, 1962.

SARAH GLEESON-WHITE ON THE PRESENCE AND FUNCTION OF MASQUERADE

In *The Member of the Wedding*, (...) Berenice observes that Frankie looks incongruous in the gaudy orange satin dress she has chosen for the wedding. It is as if "you had all your hair shaved off like a convict, and now you tie a silver ribbon around this head without any hair. It just looks peculiar.... And look at them elbows.... Here you got on this grown woman's evening dress.... And that brown crust on your elbows. The two things just don't mix" (106–7). Through such absurd mimicry of femininity, overlaid with her tomboyishness, Frankie fails to rehearse a properly feminine gender role and so reveals the approximate nature of the process.

It is Frankie's play with nomenclature that emphatically signals her donning of femininity. As earlier noted, the fact that Frankie chooses, in her assumption of the F. Jasmine identity, such a highly feminine mask and exaggerates it serves to parody the very notion of a natural and original gender. As the "connected" and romantic F. Jasmine, Frankie dreams of a future where "Captain Jarvis Addams sinks twelve Jap battleships ... [and] Mrs Janice Addams [is] elected Miss United Nations in beauty contest" (139). Now, for the first time, she listens intently to Berenice's rhetoric of love (119), and she "dressed carefully ... in her most grown and best, the pink organdie, and put on lipstick and Sweet Serenade" (61) to go about town. As F. Jasmine, she entertains a "romance" with the soldier in the Blue Moon, which makes her feel "very proper.... [S]he carefully smoothed down her dress ... so as not to sit the pleats out of the skirt" (84).

In choosing the orange satin evening dress for the wedding (106) and in wishing that she had "long bright yellow hair" (25), Frankie is undermining her attempts at femininity. It is a "not nice" dress as opposed to the "nice" pink organdie already hanging in her closet. By wishing for bright-colored hair and by preferring a gaudy dress over the more subtle and demure "good girl" dress, Frankie exaggerates "what woman wears," as does the drag queen, to make a mockery of what woman should be and "naturally" is, that is, feminine. Her clumsy attempts to become a woman underscore womanliness as performance.

At the end of *The Member of the Wedding*, after F. Jasmine's failed attempt to become a "we of me," Frankie assumes the name that embodies the installment of correct gender identification: "Frances," sensible Frances. She is "just mad about Michelangelo," reads Tennyson, and plans to become a poet herself, all acceptably feminine pursuits and ambitions. As Frances, she enters into an acceptable friendship with Mary Littlejohn. "[T]he daytime was now filled with radar, school, and Mary Littlejohn" (189), her dreams of boyish adventure now diluted to a sensible trip around the world with Mary. However, Frankie, like Mick, cannot quite carry off womanliness. She still dreams of becoming "the foremost authority on radar" (186), a typically male job at the time; her unconscious reference to two homoerotic poets—Michelangelo and Tennyson—undermines her attempt to conform to an acceptably heterosexual female identity. Furthermore, as I have already suggested, the relationship between Frances and Mary Littlejohn may not merely be one of friendship.

Frankie's parade of feminine masks, signaled by her name changes as well as her dress, parodies any notion of a fixed identity. There is no such thing here as a peeling away of masks in the hope of getting to some firm core. Beneath each mask lies another, and another. The reader is foiled at every turn in any attempt to get to the bottom of identity through Frankie's various name-crossings, dress, and behavior. Behind the sensible "Frances" is the flighty "F. Jasmine," and behind her the tomboy "Frankie." But the masquerade does not stop there for "Frankie" is another mask, of masculinity, which enacts a type of gender suspension.

(...)

Although gender may not be a matter of choice, it is nevertheless mobile, contingent, and performative. In presenting gender as a ceaseless assumption of masks, McCullers's texts disrupt any notion of stable and originary gender. What emerges from an examination of female transvestism and male cross-dressing is a suspension (albeit temporary) of either/or gender categories. The enactment of one's own gender, ideally perceived as wholly appropriate and natural, is, ironically, as much a performance as crossing over to the other gender.

Works by Carson McCullers

The Heart is a Lonely Hunter, 1940.

Reflections in a Golden Eye, 1941.

The Ballad of the Sad Café, 1943.

The Member of the Wedding, 1946.

The Ballad of the Sad Café: The Novels and Stories of Carson McCullers, 1951.

The Square Root of Wonderful (play), 1958.

Clock Without Hands, 1961.

Sweet as a Pickle, Clean as a Pig (children's poetry). Illustrated by Rolf Gerard, 1964.

The Mortgaged Heart: The Previously Uncollected Writings of Carson McCullers (Short stories, poems sketches, essays) Ed. Margarita G. Smith, 1971 (published posthumously).

Collected Stories. Introduction by Virginia Spencer Carr, 1987. (published posthumously).

Illumination and Night Glare: The Unfinished Autobiography of Carson McCullers. Eds. Carson McCullers and Carlos L. Dews, 2001.

Annotated Bibliography

Auchincloss, Lois. *Pioneers and Caretakers: A Study of 9 American Women Novelists*, University of Minnesota Press, 1965.

A critical survey of various women novelists in late nineteenth-century and the first half of the twentieth-century. Included in this examination are Sarah Orne Jewett, Edith Wharton, Ellen Glasgow, Willa Cather, Elizabeth Madox Roberts, Katherine Anne Porter, Jean Stafford, Mary McCarthy, and Carson McCullers.

"Behind the Wedding: Carson McCullers Discusses the Novel She Converted into a Stage Play." Interview with Harvey Breit. *New York Times*, January 1, 1950: sec. 2, p. 3.

An early interview with McCullers that provides a first-hand authorial account of the process of adaptation and McCullers' perspectives on writing. Contemporaneous with the premier of *The Member of the Wedding* in New York City.

Bloom, Harold. *Carson McCullers*. New York: Chelsea House Publishers, 1986.

Bloom considers the thematic, metaphoric, and structural aspects of McCullers' literary texts. Provides a critical scholarly overview of McCullers's work.

Carlton, Ann. "Beyond Gothic and Grotesque: A Feminist View of Three Female Characters of Carson McCullers." *Pembroke Magazine*. 20 (1988): 54–62.

Examines the feminist impulses found in three of Carson McCullers' works—Mick Kelly from *The Heart is a Lonely Hunter*, *The Member of the Wedding*'s Frankie Addams, and Miss Amelia from *The Ballad of the Sad Café*.

Carr, Virginia Spencer, and Millichap, Joseph R. "Carson McCullers." *American Women Writers*. Ed. Maurice Duke, Jackson R. Bryer, and M. Thomas Inge. Westport, CT: Greenwood Press, 1983, 297–319.

A bio-bibliographic essay identifying primary editions and manuscript sources of Carson McCullers, as well as secondary works including bibliography, biography, and criticism.

Carr, Virginia Spencer. *Lonely Hunter: A Biography of Carson McCullers*. Garden City, New York: Doubleday, 1975.

Widely accepted as the standard biography of Carson McCullers. Provides a detailed account of McCullers' life and work.

Clark, Charlene Kerne. "Male-Female Pairs in Carson McCullers' *The Ballad of the Sad Cafe* and *The Member of the Wedding*." *Notes on Contemporary Literature*. 9:1 (1979): 11–12.

Considers McCullers' use of characterization and the function of doubling in two of her major works.

Dusenbury, Winifred L. *The Theme of Loneliness in Modern American Drama*. Gainesville, Florida: University of Florida Press, 1960, 57–85.

Examines family relations and corresponding themes of loneliness and alienation in the stage version of McCullers' *The Member of the Wedding*.

Edmonds, Dale. *Carson McCullers*. Southern Writers Series, no. 6. Austin, Texas: Steck-Vaughn, 1969.

An early biography of the author written a few years after her death.

Evans, Oliver. *The Ballad of Carson McCullers*. New York: Coward-McCann, 1966.

The first biography written on Carson McCullers. Provides an interesting perspective on the author while she was still alive.

"'*Frankie Addams*' at 50." *Interview with Rex Reed*. New York Times, *April 16, 1967*: sec. 2, p. 15.

One of the last interviews with the author that provides a retrospective account of McCullers' life and work.

Ginsberg, Elaine. "The Female Initiation Theme in American Fiction." *Studies in American Fiction* 3, No. 1 (Spring 1975): 27–37.

Examines the theme of female initiation in American fiction, particularly as evidenced in McCullers' novels *The Member of the Wedding* and *The Heart Is a Lonely Hunter.*

Graver, Lawrence. *Carson McCullers*. Minneapolis: University of Minnesota Press, 1969.

An overview of the life and work of Carson McCullers that was published shortly after the author's death. Provides an early critical and scholarly perspective on McCullers' work.

Jackson Bryer, Kathleen Field, and Adrian Shapiro. *Carson McCullers: A Descriptive Listing and Annotated Bibliography of Criticism*. New York: Taylor & Francis, Inc., 1980.

Provides an overview of McCullers' work and a detailed listing of primary documents and secondary critical resources.

James, Judith Giblin. *Wunderkind: The Reputation of Carson McCullers*, 1940–1990. Columbia, SC: Camden House, Inc., 1995.

Traces McCullers' literary reputation through a consideration of reviews and scholarly texts related to her work. The critical and scholarly reception of McCullers's work is chronically ordered and enumerated, and these secondary sources are contextualized vis-à-vis prevailing sociopolitical and literary concerns. Provides extensive bibliography of both McCullers' publications and secondary critical sources.

Jenkins, Mackay. *The South in Black and White: Race, Sex, and Literature in the 1940s*. University of North Carolina Press, 1999.

Examines the function of race and sexuality in the works of four Southern writers—W.J. Cash, William Alexander Percy, Lillian Smith, and Carson McCullers. This text represents a social and historical consideration of Cash, Percy, Smith, and McCullers, with an emphasis on the racial politics of the 1940s.

Kiernan, Robert. *Katherine Anne Porter and Carson McCullers: A Reference Guide*. New York: G.K. Hall & Co., 1976.

Examines the work of Porter and McCullers from both a critical and biographical standpoint. Includes a bibliography of scholarly resources on both authors.

Kumar, Anil. *Alienation in the Fiction of Carson McCullers, J.D. Salinger, and James Purdy*. Amritsar: Guru Nanack Dev University, 1991.

Investigates the theme of alienation in the works of McCullers, Salinger, and Purdy and provides a theoretical and comparative frame upon which to consider each writer.

Rich, Nancy B. *Flowering Dream: The Historical Saga of Carson McCullers*.

Considers McCullers's literary productions from the standpoint of biography and history. The primary argument behind this study is that McCullers' literary imagination was connected to the historical realities in which she was situated.

Savigneau, Josyane (translated by Joan E. Howard). *Carson McCullers: A Life*, Boston: Houghton Mifflin, 2001.

A biographical account of Carson McCullers' life and career. The first biographer to have the full cooperation of the McCullers estate, Savigneau includes relatively new perspectives and previously undisclosed details of McCullers' life and work.

Walker, Brannon Sue. *It's Good Weather for Fudge: Conversing with Carson McCullers*. New South Inc, 2003.

A book-length narrative poem in which the poet imagines a friendship and conversation with McCullers. Though a fictionalized account, Walker does make many allusions to the life and works of Carson McCullers and represents a biography in poetic form.

Weaks, Mary Louise and Carolyn Perry. *Southern Women's Writing: Colonial to Contemporary*. Gainesville: University Press of Florida, 1995.

An exhaustive and comprehensive anthology of Southern women's writing that includes letters, journal and diary entries, essays, poetry, and fiction. Historically ordered, each section includes both an introduction to the period and a biography of the author. McCullers is included in the "Modern South" section of the text.

White, Barbara A. *Growing Up Female: Adolescent Girlhood in American Fiction, Vol. 59*. Greenwood Publishing Group Incorporated, 1985.

Examines the thematic focus on female adolescence in American literature. This text reconsiders the coming-of-age narrative from a feminist perspective, and includes both general surveys and in-depth investigations of works by Edith Wharton, Ruth Suckow, Jean Stafford, and Carson McCullers.

Wikborg, Eleanor. *Carson McCullers'* The Member of the Wedding: *Aspects of Structure and Style*. Göteborg: Acta Universitatis Gothoburgensis, 1975.

Provides a close literary reading of *The Member of the Wedding* and focuses on the structural and allegorical elements in the novella.

Contributors

Harold Bloom is Sterling Professor of the Humanities at Yale University. He is the author of over 20 books, including *Shelley's Mythmaking* (1959), *The Visionary Company* (1961), *Blake's Apocalypse* (1963), *Yeats* (1970), *A Map of Misreading* (1975), *Kabbalah and Criticism* (1975), *Agon: Toward a Theory of Revisionism* (1982), *The American Religion* (1992), *The Western Canon* (1994), and *Omens of Millennium: The Gnosis of Angels, Dreams, and Resurrection* (1996). *The Anxiety of Influence* (1973) sets forth Professor Bloom's provocative theory of the literary relationships between the great writers and their predecessors. His most recent books include *Shakespeare: The Invention of the Human* (1998), a 1998 National Book Award finalist, *How to Read and Why* (2000), *Genius: A Mosaic of One Hundred Exemplary Creative Minds* (2002), and *Hamlet: Poem Unlimited* (2003). In 1999, Professor Bloom received the prestigious American Academy of Arts and Letters Gold Medal for Criticism, and in 2002 he received the Catalonia International Prize.

Cathy Schlund-Vials is a Ph.D. candidate in the American Studies Program in the Department of English at the University of Massachusetts-Amherst. Her fields of research include twentieth-century immigration narratives, Ethnic Studies, whiteness studies, and Asian American Studies. She is currently the Program Curator for New WORLD Theater, a multicultural theater company in residence at the University of Massachusetts. She was also the recipient of the 2002–2003 Distinguished Teaching Award at the University of Massachusetts-Amherst.

George Dangerfield (1904–1986) was born in England, educated at Oxford, and served as the literary editor of *Vanity Fair* in the early 1930s. Mr. Dangerfield lectured widely and wrote numerous reviews and articles for the *New York Times Book Review*, *The New Republic*, and the *Saturday Review*. His scholarly texts include *Bengal Mutiny: The Story of the Sepoy Rebellion*, *The Strange Death of Liberal England*, *Victoria's Heir: The Education of a Prince*, *Chancellor Robert R. Livingston of New York*, *The Awakening of American Nationalism, 1815–1828*, *Defiance to the Old World: The Story Behind the Monroe Doctrine* (1970), and *The Damnable Question: A Study in Anglo-Irish Relations* (1976). His work, *Era of Good Feelings*, won the 1952 Pulitzer Prize for history.

Robert S. Philips is a prize-winning poet, fiction writer, critic and teacher who is John and Rebecca Moores University Scholar at the University of Houston. Mr. Phillips has received an Award in Literature and Creative Writing from The American Academy of Arts and Letters, a CAPS Grant from the New York State Council on the Arts, a National Public Radio Fiction Prize, a Pushcart Prize, and the Enron Teaching Excellence Award. He has received fellowships from Yaddo, the MacDowell Colony, and the Djerassi Foundation (among others). Mr. Phillips is the author and editor of twenty-seven books, three of which were named a "Memorable Book of the Year" by the *New York Times*, and he is Councilor of the Texas Institute of Letters.

Richard M. Cook received his Ph.D. in English from the University of Michigan and is currently an Associate Professor in the Department of English at the University of Missouri-St. Louis. He is the author of *Carson McCullers*.

Margaret B. McDowell is Professor of Rhetoric at the University of Iowa. She served as the first chairperson of the Women's Studies Program at the University of Iowa, and has been on the executive committees for the Women's Caucus for the Modern Languages and for the Midwest Modern Language Association. She received her M.A. in creative writing and a Ph.D. in English from the University of Iowa. She is the author of *Edith Wharton* and *Carson McCullers* in the Twayne United States Authors series, and she has written articles on the rhetoric of contemporary feminism, the teaching of language arts to children, children's literature, college composition, Southern women writers, and African American women writers.

Louise Westling is a Professor in the English Department at the University of Oregon. Her areas of interest include twentieth-century American fiction, autobiography, and ecocriticism, and her current work considers the intersections of science and cultural studies. Dr. Westling's publications include *Sacred Groves and Ravaged Gardens: The Fiction of Eudora Welty, Carson McCullers, and Flannery O'Connor* and *The Green Breast of the New World: Landscape, Gender, and American Fiction*. She was an editor for *He Included Me: The Autobiography of Sara Rice* and David Frost, Jr.'s *Witness to Injustice*. Recent articles by Dr. Westling include "Women, Landscape, and the Legacy of Gilgamesh in *Absalom, Absalom!* and *Go Down Moses*" and "Flannery O'Connor's Hilarious Rage."

Kenneth Chamlee is the Iva Bunch Seese Distinguished Professor of English at Brevard College in Brevard, North Carolina, where he also served as the 1998–2000 Johnie H. Jones Distinguished Professor of Teaching. Dr. Chamlee received his Ph.D. in English at the University of North Carolina at Greensboro. His areas of interest include modern poetry, creative writing, American and British Literature.

Virginia Spencer Carr is the John B. and Elena Diaz-Verson Amos Distinguished Chair in English Letters at Georgia State University in Atlanta, Georgia. Dr. Carr's first book, *The Lonely Hunter: A Biography of Carson McCullers*, was awarded the Francis Butler Simkins Prize of the Southern Historical Society and Longwood College for "distinguished writing in Southern history," and her second book, *Dos Passos: A Life* was selected "best book of nonfiction" for 1984 by the Dixie Council of Authors and Journalists. Dr. Carr holds an honorary doctorate in humane letters (Lynchburg College) and is a recipient of a Georgia Governor's Award in the Humanities. She was a Senior Fulbright Professor at the University of Wroclaw,

Poland (1980) and she held the 1993 Stanley J. Kahrl Fellowship in Theater History at Harvard University. Dr. Carr is also the editor of *Katherine Anne Porter's 'Flowering Judas': Text, Essays, and Criticism* and her profile appears in the 1992 *Dictionary of Literary Biography, Twentieth Century*.

Thadious M. Davis is the Gertrude Conaway Vanderbilt Professor of English of Vanderbilt University. Her research interests include 20th Century American Literature, African American Literature, Southern American Literature, and Women's Literature. A former editor of *The Langston Hughes Review*, Dr. Davis is coeditor of the Gender and American Culture Series, University of North Carolina Press. She is the author of *Nella Larsen, Novelist of the Harlem Renaissance* (1994) and *Faulkner's "Negro": Art and the Southern Context* (1982), and the editor of numerous reference texts. Dr. Davis is currently a fellow at the New York Public Library's Center for Scholars and Writers. She was recently the R. Stanton Avery Distinguished Fellow at the Huntington Library, where she completed her latest book, *Games of Property: Race, Gender, Law and Faulkner's Go Down Moses* (Duke University Press, 2002).

Tony Jason Stafford is a Professor and the Chair of the English Department at the University of Texas at El Paso. He received his Ph.D. from Louisiana State University with a specialty in Renaissance literature and drama and a dissertation on "Shakespeare's Use of the Sea." Dr. Stafford has published scholarly articles and Shakespeare and other Renaissance dramatists as well as on George Bernard Shaw, David Mamet, David Rabe, and other modern British and American dramatists. He is also a playwright who has had plays produced in such places as Philadelphia, Washington, D.C.; Bloomington, Indiana; Houston, Denver, Hollywood, El Paso, and Las Cruces. Over the last several years, Dr. Stafford has had three of his plays produced at the World Premiere Theatre in Eureka, CA and has just finished his first novel, *The Grace of a Summer's Day*.

Sarah GleesonWhite is an independent scholar living in Sydney, Australia. She is the author of *Strange Bodies: Gender and Identity in the Novels of Carson McCullers*.

Acknowledgments

First and foremost, I would like to extend a special and sincere thank you to Sue Naab at Chelsea House Publishers for her advice, quick responses, and guidance. I would also like to give my most heartfelt appreciation to my husband, Christopher Vials, for his keen editorial sense, incredible patience, and sense of humor.

"An Adolescent's Four Days" by George Dangerfield. From *Critical Essays on Carson McCullers*. Eds. Beverly Lyon Clark and Melvin J. Friedman. New York: G.K. Hall & Co., 1996. pp. 31–33. (Originally appeared in the *Saturday Review*, 30 March 1946). Reprinted by permission.

"The Gothic Architecture of *The Member of the Wedding*" by Robert S. Phillips. From *Renascence: Essays on Values in Literature*, Vol. XVI, No. 2, Winter, 1964. pp. 59–72. Reprinted by permission.

"*The Member of the Wedding*" by Richard M. Cook. From *Carson McCullers*. Modern Literature Monographs. New York: Ungar Publishing Co., 1975. pp. 59–81. Reprinted by permission.

"*The Member of the Wedding*" by Margaret B. McDowell. From *Carson McCullers*. Boston: Twayne Publishers, 1980. pp. 80–95. Reprinted by permission.

"Tomboys and Revolting Femininity" by Louise Westling. From *Sacred Groves and Ravaged Gardens: The Fiction of Eudora Welty, Carson McCullers, and Flannery O' Connor*. Athens, GA: Georgia UP, 1985. pp. 110–132. Reprinted by permission.

"Cafes and Community in Three McCullers Novels" by Kenneth D. Chamlee. From *Studies in American Fiction* 18 (Autumn 1990): 233–40. Reprinted by permission.

"*The Member of the Wedding*" by Virginia Spencer Carr. From *Understanding Carson McCullers*. University of South Carolina Press, 1990. pp. 72–87. Reprinted by permission.

"'Gray Eyes is Glass': Image and Theme in *The Member of the Wedding*" by Tony J. Stafford. From *American Drama* 3 (Fall 1993): 54–66. Reprinted by permission.

"Erasing the 'We of Me' and Rewriting the Racial Script: Carson McCullers's Two *Member(s) of the Wedding*" by Thadious M. Davis. From *Critical Essays on Carson McCullers*. Eds. Beverly Lyon Clark and Melvin J. Friedman. New York: G.K. Hall & Co., 1996. pp. 206–219. Reprinted by permission.

"The Masquerade: *The Heart is a Lonely Hunter*, *The Member of the Wedding*, and *The Ballad of the Sad Café*" by Sarah Gleeson-White. From *Strange Bodies: Gender and Identity in the Novels of Carson McCullers*. Alabama UP, 2003. pp. 68–95. Reprinted by permission.

Index